Behavior
Therapy

Theories of Psychotherapy Series

Theories of Psychotherapy Series
Jon Carlson and Matt Englar-Carlson, Series Editors

Behavior
Therapy

Martin M. Antony and Lizabeth Roemer

American Psychological Association

Washington, DC

Published by
American Psychological Association
750 First Street, NE
Washington, DC 20002
www.apa.org

To order
APA Order Department
P.O. Box 92984
Washington, DC 20090-2984
Tel: (800) 374-2721; Direct: (202) 336-5510
Fax: (202) 336-5502; TDD/TTY: (202) 336-6123
Online: www.apa.org/books/
E-mail: order@apa.org

In the U.K., Europe, Africa, and the Middle East, copies may be ordered from
American Psychological Association
3 Henrietta Street
Covent Garden, London
WC2E 8LU England

Typeset in Minion by Circle Graphics, Columbia, MD

Printer: United Book Press, Baltimore, MD
Cover Designer: Minker Design, Sarasota, FL
Cover Art: *Lily Rising*, 2005, oil and mixed media on panel in craquelure frame, by Betsy Bauer

The opinions and statements published are the responsibility of the authors, and such opinions and statements do not necessarily represent the policies of the American Psychological Association.

Library of Congress Cataloging-in-Publication Data

Antony, Martin M.
  Behavior therapy / Martin M. Antony and Lizabeth Roemer. — 1st ed.
    p. ; cm. — (Theories of psychotherapy series)
  Includes bibliographical references and index.
  ISBN-13: 978-1-4338-0984-2
  ISBN-10: 1-4338-0984-2
  1. Behavior therapy. I. Roemer, Lizabeth, 1967- II. American Psychological Association. III. Title. IV. Series: Theories of psychotherapy series.
    [DNLM: 1. Behavior Therapy. WM 425]
  RC489.B4A58 2011
  616.89'142—dc22
                                        2011005861

British Library Cataloguing-in-Publication Data
A CIP record is available from the British Library.

Printed in the United States of America
First Edition

For Cynthia
—*Martin M. Antony*

For my mentor, Tom Borkovec
—*Lizabeth Roemer*

Contents

Series Preface

Some might argue that in the contemporary clinical practice of psychotherapy, evidence-based intervention and effective outcome have overshadowed theory in importance. Maybe. But, as the editors of this series, we don't propose to take up that controversy here. We do know that psychotherapists adopt and practice according to one theory or another because their experience, and decades of good evidence, suggests that having a sound theory of psychotherapy leads to greater therapeutic success. Still, the role of theory in the helping process can be hard to explain. This narrative about solving problems helps convey theory's importance:

> Aesop tells the fable of the sun and wind having a contest to decide who was the most powerful. From above the earth, they spotted a man walking down the street, and the wind said that he bet he could get the man's coat off. The sun agreed to the contest. The wind blew and the man held on tightly to his coat. The more the wind blew, the tighter he held. The sun said it was his turn. He put all of his energy into creating warm sunshine, and soon the man took off his coat.

What does a competition between the sun and the wind to remove a man's coat have to do with theories of psychotherapy? We think this deceptively simple story highlights the importance of theory as the precursor to any effective intervention—and hence to a favorable outcome. Without a guiding theory we might treat the symptom without understanding the role of the individual. Or we might create power conflicts with our clients and not understand that, at times, indirect means of helping (sunshine) are often as effective—if not more so—than direct ones (wind). In the absence of theory, we might lose track of the treatment rationale and instead get caught up in, for example, social correctness and not wanting to do something that looks too simple.

What exactly *is* theory? The *APA Dictionary of Psychology* defines theory as "a principle or body of interrelated principles that purports to explain or predict a number of interrelated phenomena." In psychotherapy, a theory is a set of principles used to explain human thought and behavior, including what causes people to change. In practice, a theory creates the goals of therapy and specifies how to pursue them. Haley (1997) noted that a theory of psychotherapy ought to be simple enough for the average therapist to understand, but comprehensive enough to account for a wide range of eventualities. Furthermore, a theory guides action toward successful outcomes while generating hope in both the therapist and client that recovery is possible.

Theory is the compass that allows psychotherapists to navigate the vast territory of clinical practice. In the same ways that navigational tools have been modified to adapt to advances in thinking and ever-expanding territories to explore, theories of psychotherapy have changed over time. The different schools of theories are commonly referred to as waves, the first wave being psychodynamic theories (i.e., Adlerian, psychoanalytic), the second wave learning theories (i.e., behavioral, cognitive–behavioral), the third wave humanistic theories (person-centered, gestalt, existential), the fourth wave feminist and multicultural theories, and the fifth wave postmodern and constructivist theories. In many ways, these waves represent how psychotherapy has adapted and responded to changes in psychology, society, and epistemology, as well as to changes in the nature of psychotherapy itself. Psychotherapy and the theories that guide it are dynamic and responsive. The wide variety of theories is also testament to the different ways in which the same human behavior can be conceptualized (Frew & Spiegler, 2008).

It is with these two concepts in mind—the central importance of theory and the natural evolution of theoretical thinking—that we developed the Theories of Psychotherapy Series. Both of us are thoroughly fascinated by theory and the range of complex ideas that drive each model. As university faculty members who teach courses on the theories of psychotherapy, we wanted to create learning materials that not only highlight the essence of the major theories for professionals and professionals in training but also clearly bring the reader up to date on the current status of the models. Often in books on theory, the biography of the original theorist overshadows the evolution of the model. In contrast, our intent is to highlight the contemporary uses of the theories as well as their history and context.

As this project began, we faced two immediate decisions: which theories to address and who best to present them. We looked at graduate-level theories of psychotherapy courses to see which theories are being taught, and we explored popular scholarly books, articles, and conferences to determine which theories draw the most interest. We then developed a dream list of authors from among the best minds in contemporary theoretical practice. Each author is one of the leading proponents of that approach as well as a knowledgeable practitioner. We asked each author to review the core constructs of the theory, bring the theory into the modern sphere of clinical practice by looking at it through a context of evidence-based practice, and clearly illustrate how the theory looks in action.

There are 24 titles planned for the series. Each title can stand alone or can be put together with a few other titles to create materials for a course in psychotherapy theories. This option allows instructors to create a course featuring the approaches they believe are the most salient today. To support this end, APA Books has also developed a DVD for each of the approaches that demonstrates the theory in practice with a real client. Many of the DVDs show therapy over six sessions. Contact APA Books for a complete list of available DVD programs (http://www.apa.org/pubs/videos).

Behavior therapy stands as one of the most influential and easily recognizable forms of psychotherapy. Rather than one set of treatments, behavior therapy includes a variety of behavior therapies that are focused on changing and learning new behaviors. In *Behavior Therapy*, Martin Antony and Lizabeth Roemer clearly outline the core constructs that unify behavioral therapies and show the evolution of behavioral treatment from the past into contemporary practice. Along the way, the authors note how the practice of behavior therapy has remained in step with advances in research and empirical science. Whereas the reader might expect the book to solidly place behavior therapy as a form of evidence-based practice for many presenting concerns, the authors do a masterful job in outlining how behavior therapists modify their approach and treatment strategies to be in alignment with a client's cultural identity. Overall, we thoroughly enjoyed reading this book and repeatedly found ourselves in alignment with the perspective of the authors. Though behavior therapy stands as one of the classic approaches to therapy, we are sure that readers of this book will find something new and enlightening in looking at the contemporary use of behavior therapy.

—*Jon Carlson and Matt Englar-Carlson*

REFERENCES

Frew, J., & Spiegler, M. (2008). *Contemporary psychotherapies for a diverse world.* Boston, MA: Lahaska Press.

Haley, J. (1997). *Leaving home: The therapy of disturbed young people.* New York, NY: Routledge.

How to Use This Book With APA Psychotherapy Videos

Each book in the Theories of Psychotherapy Series is specifically paired with a DVD that demonstrates the theory applied in actual therapy with a real client. Many DVDs feature the author of the book as the guest therapist, allowing students to see an eminent scholar and practitioner putting the theory he or she writes about into action.

The DVDs have a number of features that make them excellent tools for learning more about theoretical concepts:

- Many DVDs contain six full sessions of psychotherapy over time, giving viewers a chance to see how clients respond to the application of the theory over the course of several sessions.
- Each DVD has a brief introductory discussion recapping the basic features of the theory behind the approach demonstrated. This allows viewers to review the key aspects of the approach about which they have just read.
- DVDs feature actual clients in unedited psychotherapy sessions. This provides a unique opportunity to get a sense of the look and feel of real psychotherapy, something that written case examples and transcripts cannot always convey.
- There is a therapist commentary track that viewers may choose to play during the psychotherapy sessions. This track gives unique insight into why therapists do what they do in a session.
- Further, it provides an in vivo opportunity to see how the therapist uses the model to conceptualize the client.

The books and DVDs together make a powerful teaching tool for showing how theoretical principles affect practice. In the case of this book, the DVD *Behavioral Therapy Over Time* features coauthor Martin M. Antony as the guest expert who provides a vivid example of how this approach looks in practice. In the six sessions featured on this DVD, Antony works with a female client who suffers from compulsive hoarding. Over the course of therapy, Antony explores ways of overcoming this behavior, including exposure to discarding unneeded items and learning alternative responses to the urge to hoard, and the client begins to learn how she has control over what had seemed to be a compulsive behavior.

Acknowledgments

Thank you to Jon Carlson and Matt Englar-Carlson for inviting us to write this book and to Ed Meidenbauer at the American Psychological Association for his support throughout the editorial process. We also thank Cara Fuchs, Sarah Hayes-Skelton, Sue Orsillo, and Mike Treanor for helpful comments on specific sections of the manuscript, and Josh Bartok, Sarah Hayes-Skelton, and David Pantalone for support during the writing process. Finally, thank you to Jenny Rogojanski for her assistance in reviewing the final manuscript for publication.

Behavior
Therapy

1

Introduction

Behavior therapy is not a single, cohesive approach to treatment. Rather, behavior therapy is both varied and evolving, and therapists differ with respect to the strategies they use and their assumptions about the best ways to change problem behaviors. In fact, Bellack and Hersen (1985) identified more than 150 behavioral treatments in their *Dictionary of Behavior Therapy Techniques,* and many additional strategies have been developed and tested since the publication of their compendium more than 25 years ago. Behavior therapists use a wide range of techniques, including reinforcement-based approaches, cognitive restructuring, exposure to feared situations, mindfulness meditation, relaxation training, problem-solving training, behavioral rehearsal, biofeedback, and many others. Behavior therapists also differ in the extent to which they rely on standard, session-by-session, evidence-based treatment protocols rather than a more individualized approach to selecting target behaviors and strategies that are tailored to their clients' specific needs (G. T. Wilson, 1998).

Behavioral perspectives on the causes of psychopathology also vary among therapists. For example, therapists trained in an operant conditioning tradition (sometimes referred to as *radical behaviorism*) presuppose that all behavior has a function and that both adaptive and maladaptive behaviors stem from patterns of reinforcement and punishment in the environment. This approach assumes that by altering environmental contingencies, a therapist can facilitate changes in an individual's behavior. Other behavior therapists might focus more on the role of learned associations, such as learning fear in response to a given context because something threatening happened in that context, and help clients to form new, nonthreatening associations to these fear cues. Still other behavior therapists may incorporate cognitive strategies in their work and see individuals' maladaptive beliefs, assumptions, and predictions as one source of clinical problems. These therapists might directly address these beliefs and assumptions in treatment or encourage new behaviors in order to challenge these beliefs. Often, therapists fall along a continuum of these approaches or draw from all of them.

Although behavior therapists differ significantly in their approaches to treatment, behavior therapy has important characteristics that are shared across behavioral perspectives and that distinguish it from other therapeutic modalities. These characteristics include the following:

- *The focus of behavior therapy is on changing behavior.* The goals of behavior therapy include increasing the frequency of adaptive behaviors, decreasing the frequency of maladaptive behaviors, and enhancing flexibility in the individual's behavioral repertoire. In behavior therapy, the term *behavior* refers to a wide range of responses, including overt motor behaviors, cognitions, emotions, and physiological responses. Because the goals of behavior therapy are framed in the context of specific behaviors (e.g., decreasing the frequency of panic attacks, increasing social skills, eliminating bed wetting, enhancing relationship satisfaction), outcomes can be readily measured, in contrast to approaches with goals such as "enhancing personal growth" or "increasing insight," which are more difficult to operationalize and measure.
- *Behaviors are seen as functional.* From a behavioral perspective, all problem behaviors make sense in that they are associated with some type of desired consequence (often an immediate reduction in distress) or are the result of learned associations based on experiences, modeling, or

instruction. By seeing behaviors as understandable, behaviorists refrain from blaming clients for their problems and help them to understand their own responses and learn new ways of responding.

■ *Behavior therapy is rooted in empiricism.* Behavior therapists adopt an empirical approach to therapy. They generate specific hypotheses regarding the variables that are presumed to maintain target behaviors, and they collect data to assess the validity of their hypotheses. They also evaluate the effects of their interventions throughout the course of treatment, using empirically validated measures, where available.

■ *Behavioral treatments are well supported by research.* Although behavior therapy is not the only therapeutic modality to be supported by empirical research, most randomized controlled trials evaluating psychological treatments for specific disorders have been based on some type of behavioral intervention (for a review, see Chapter 5).

■ *Behavior therapy is active.* Behavioral strategies typically involve having the client perform some action, such as monitoring activities or thoughts, or engage in some new activity or practice. For example, a client learning to manage stress might practice progressive muscle relaxation during weekly treatment sessions, as well as practicing on a daily basis between therapy visits. Also, relative to practitioners of other therapies, behavior therapists are directive, frequently offering advice and suggestions to the client and collaborating in the planning of homework practices. In fact, much of the therapeutic change that occurs in behavior therapy is assumed to be a result of behavioral practices that occur between therapy sessions.

■ *Behavior therapy emphasizes variables that maintain behavior.* Although behavior therapy acknowledges the importance of past events in the early development of problem behavior, past history is assumed to have a much smaller role in the maintenance of behavior over time. For example, in a client with posttraumatic stress disorder after an assault, a behavior therapist would likely use strategies to change behaviors that are assumed to maintain the client's problems currently, such as exposure (to reduce avoidance of feared situations, memories, and emotions), cognitive restructuring (to shift maladaptive beliefs about the trauma and related cues), mindfulness practice (to help clients to experience and accept unpleasant feelings rather than trying to control them), or progressive muscle relaxation (to reduce heightened physiological arousal). Relative to some other therapies, behavior therapy is much less likely to focus on the effects of early developmental events on the later development of psychopathology.

- *Behavior therapy is transparent.* In most cases, the theoretical rationale for behavioral treatments is articulated to clients clearly, and clients are provided with a thorough understanding of the strategies they are using and the reasons for using each strategy.
- *Behavior therapy is time limited.* Relative to some other forms of therapy, behavioral treatments are typically brief, often lasting 10 to 20 sessions. Treatments for more focused problems (e.g., Öst's [1997] single-session treatment for specific phobias) may be even briefer, whereas treatments for more complex problems often last longer (e.g., dialectical behavior therapy for borderline personality disorder may last a year or longer; Linehan et al., 2006).

The breadth and complexity of behavior therapy continue to develop and increase. What was once a somewhat cohesive approach to intervention has evolved into a number of overlapping yet distinct approaches to psychotherapy, including operant conditioning–based treatments, cognitive–behavioral therapy, dialectical behavior therapy, and acceptance and commitment therapy, to name a few. This book provides an overview of behavior therapy, including its historical and theoretical foundations, the range of strategies and techniques that are used, and the evidence regarding its effectiveness.

2

History

Behavior therapy was first established as a school of psychotherapy around the middle of the 20th century. Its origins are complex and were influenced by a wide range of factors, including a proliferation of experimental research and theory related to learning processes and dissatisfaction with psychoanalysis, the most popular approach to treating psychopathology at that time. The field of psychology was primed to embrace a more scientific approach to understanding and treating psychological problems with the establishment of the scientist–practitioner training model, which began with the Boulder Conference on Graduate Education in Clinical Psychology in 1949 and emphasized the importance of training clinical psychologists as both scientists and practitioners (Benjamin & Baker, 2000). Although there were attempts to reconcile psychoanalysis with learning theory (e.g., Dollard & Miller, 1950), many psychologists began to abandon psychoanalysis in favor of approaches that could be more easily subjected to scientific study in the laboratory.

ORIGINS

Although formal behavior therapy is only a few decades old, there is evidence that several of the strategies that are part of contemporary behavior therapy were used well before the systematic development and study of behavioral treatments. For example, about 2,000 years ago a Roman scholar named Gaius Plinius Secundus (or Pliny the Elder) treated alcoholism by putting spiders at the bottom of a drinker's glass—a variation on what might now be called *aversion therapy* (Franks, 1963). Similarly, strategies resembling modeling, shaping, and reinforcement were used by French medical student Jean-Marc-Gaspard Itard (1962) to rehabilitate Victor of Aveyron (also known as the Wild Boy of Aveyron), a child who grew up in the late 18th century with no human contact until about the age of 12. Even Freud (1919/1950) and Janet (1925) advocated for the use of exposure-based behavioral approaches in some of their writings. Although a handful of accounts such as these exist in the literature, there is no evidence that these early writings had any impact on the development of behavior therapy. Rather, the founders of behavior therapy credited early learning theorists, such as Clark Hull, Ivan Pavlov, B. F. Skinner, Edward Thorndike, John Watson, and others, for their inspiration.

In the early 1900s, Pavlov conducted a series of experiments showing that dogs could learn to salivate in response to a previously neutral stimulus (e.g., a light, a tone) after repeatedly pairing food with the neutral stimulus. This process came to be known as *classical conditioning* (although it is also sometimes called *Pavlovian conditioning* or *respondent conditioning;* Pavlov, 1927). John B. Watson popularized the work of Pavlov and first began to apply classical conditioning principles to problems of human behavior. For example, Watson and Raynor's (1920) famous case study demonstrated how an infant named Albert could be taught to fear a white rat by pairing the presence of the rat with a loud noise. Watson was an experimental psychologist based at Johns Hopkins University, and he is generally credited with founding the psychological school known as *behaviorism* (Watson, 1913). Watson believed in studying only observable behaviors, and he rejected suggestions that unobservable experiences, such as thoughts or emotions, should be the focus of study in psychology.

In the 1920s and 1930s, interventions based on behavioral principles began to emerge. For example, in 1924 Mary Cover Jones (a student of Watson's) published a report of her successful treatment of a boy named Peter who feared rabbits. The treatment involved having Peter observe other children comfortably playing with rabbits, combined with gradually approaching (and eventually touching) rabbits until he was no longer frightened (Jones, 1924). This case was one of the earliest descriptions of behavioral strategies known as *modeling* and *in vivo exposure,* both of which continue to be used today. Several years later, Yale University psychologists Orval Hobart Mowrer and Willie Mae Mowrer (1938) developed the bell and pad, a behavioral treatment for bedwetting that was based on classical conditioning principles. Essentially, the treatment involves placing under a child's sheets a moisture-sensitive pad that triggers the ringing of a bell when the child urinates, thereby waking up the child. Over time, the sound of the bell becomes associated with the experience of urinating, and the child learns to wake up in response to the urge to urinate, even before he or she loses bladder control. The bell and pad is still considered to be the treatment of choice for bedwetting in children (Mellon, 2005).

In addition to the work of Pavlov, Hull, Watson, Mowrer, and others in classical or respondent conditioning, early behavioral theorists also studied instrumental or operant conditioning paradigms. For example, Edward Thorndike's (1911) writings on the law of effect discussed the ways in which the frequency of behavior can be increased or decreased by changing its consequences (i.e., reinforcement and punishment). For example, a child's temper tantrums might be maintained through positive reinforcement by the attention he or she receives for the outbursts. Thorndike was the first to discuss the process of operant conditioning, although B. F. Skinner (1938) and his colleagues would later develop these ideas further. It was the work of Thorndike, Skinner, and other operant theorists that had the biggest impact on the development of behavior therapy in the United States.

BEHAVIOR THERAPY IN THE 1950s AND 1960s

Behavior therapy emerged simultaneously in South Africa, the United Kingdom, the United States, and Canada in the 1950s and 1960s (Franks, 2001; Lazarus, 2001). In South Africa, Joseph Wolpe (a medical student at the time) was encouraged by psychologists James Taylor, Cynthia Adelstein, and Leo Reyna to study classical conditioning and learning theory, and during this time he began his famous studies on conditioning processes in cats (e.g., Wolpe, 1952). After receiving his MD degree in 1948, Wolpe initially worked full time in private practice in Johannesburg, although he subsequently began training students at the University of Witwatersrand, including Arnold Lazarus and Stanley Rachman, who soon became behavior therapy pioneers in their own right. Wolpe remained in Johannesburg until 1960, when he accepted a position at the University of Virginia School of Medicine. Wolpe was one of the first individuals to study exposure-based treatments for phobias. He is perhaps best known for developing *systematic desensitization*—a therapy based on his theory of reciprocal inhibition that combines exposure to mental images of a feared object or situation with progressive muscle relaxation (Wolpe, 1958). Wolpe also cofounded the *Journal of Behavior Therapy and Experimental Psychiatry* with his mentor, Leo Reyna. Lazarus completed his PhD under Wolpe's supervision and took over Wolpe's private practice when Wolpe moved to the United States (Lazarus, 2001). In 1963, Lazarus spent a year as a visiting assistant professor of psychology at Stanford University and returned to the United States in 1966, where he has remained ever since. In the early 1970s, Lazarus developed multimodal therapy, an integrative behavioral treatment that includes cognitive strategies and elements of other approaches.

Around the same time that Wolpe was active in South Africa, Hans Eysenck assembled a team of clinical researchers at the Institute of Psychiatry (Maudsley Hospital) in London. His group included several behavior therapy pioneers, such as Cyril Franks and Stanley Rachman, who completed his PhD under Eysenck's supervision at the University of London after leaving Wolpe's group in South Africa (Rachman eventually moved to the University of British Columbia in Canada). In 1963, Eysenck founded the first major journal in behavior therapy, called *Behaviour Research and Therapy* (or *BRAT,* as it is affectionately known), which remains one of the highest-impact journals in clinical psychology. When Eysenck retired, Rachman took over as editor, and G. Terence Wilson has since assumed that position.

In 1957, Cyril Franks left Eysenck's group to accept a position as director of psychology at the Neuropsychiatric Institute, Princeton, New Jersey. In 1966, Franks founded the Association for Advancement of the Behavioral Therapies (AABT) and served as the association's first president. Other founding members included John Paul Brady, Joseph Cautela, Edward Dengrove, Martin Gittelman, Leonard Krasner, Arnold Lazarus, Andrew Salter, Dorothy Susskind, and Joseph Wolpe. Franks also launched *Behavior Therapy* (AABT's official journal) and served as its founding editor. In 1967, AABT changed its name to the Association for Advancement of Behavior Therapy, and in 2005, the association's name was changed again, to the Association for Behavioral and Cognitive Therapies (ABCT). With almost 5,000 members, ABCT is North America's largest association for researchers, practitioners, and students with an interest in behavioral treatments.

As reviewed by Lazarus (2001), behavior therapy in South Africa and England was influenced mostly by respondent conditioning theory (e.g., Pavlovian approaches), whereas in North America, behavioral treatments were most closely aligned with the operant conditioning approaches of B. F. Skinner. Nathan Azrin (a former student of Skinner's) was a pioneer in establishing the field of applied behavior analysis and developed a wide range of treatments based on operant conditioning, including reinforcement-based treatments for substance use disorders. Another North American pioneer was Teodoro Ayllon, who conducted studies in the late 1950s at the Saskatchewan Hospital in Canada, showing that operant principles could be used to change dysfunctional behaviors in patients with serious mental illness (e.g., Ayllon, 1963). Ayllon and Azrin collaborated on a number of studies and books describing their behavioral treatment known as *token economy,* a method in which desired behaviors are reinforced by giving an individual tokens that can later be exchanged for rewards (e.g., Ayllon & Azrin, 1965, 1968).

According to Lazarus (2001), Wolpe and his group had been using the term *conditioning therapy* to describe their approach to treatment. At a team meeting in 1957, Lazarus suggested that they replace the term *conditioning therapy* with *behavior therapy* and that they start to refer to themselves as *behavior therapists*. Although Wolpe continued to use the term *conditioning therapy* for the next few years (e.g., Wolpe, Salter, & Reyna, 1964), Lazarus (1958) was the first to use the terms *behavior therapy* and *behavior therapist* in a journal article. However, unbeknownst to Lazarus, the term *behavior therapy* had been used previously by Lindsley, Skinner, and Solomon (1953) in a mimeographed status report on operant conditioning with psychotic inpatients at Metropolitan State Hospital, Waltham, Massachusetts (Lindsley, 2001). Eysenck (1959) independently used these terms in print as well, and he popularized the term *behavior therapy* in his 1960 and 1964 books on the subject. Although the phrase *behavior therapy* was popular outside of the United States, the expression *behavior modification* was initially more commonly used in the United States, although this has changed over time.

CONTEMPORARY BEHAVIOR THERAPY: EVOLUTION TO THE PRESENT

Almost from its inception, the boundaries of behavior therapy began to expand. Perhaps the most influential change in traditional behavioral treatments was the incorporation of cognitive strategies, initially by psychologist Albert Ellis. Ellis began his career as a clinical sexologist, using techniques based on the work of several early 20th-century physicians, including Iwan Bloch (1908), August Forel (1922), Havelock Ellis (1936), and W. F. Robie (1925). According to Albert Ellis (2001), these strategies were directive and had much in common with techniques that would later become part of cognitive–behavioral therapy (CBT), such as psychoeducation, in vivo homework assignments, and strategies for reducing beliefs associated with shame and guilt. Ellis was also inspired by the work of John Watson and colleagues and apparently used a desensitization-based treatment on himself to overcome a fear of public speaking (A. Ellis,

2001). Ellis used these strategies with his clients from 1943 to 1947, before becoming trained as a psychoanalyst and practicing neo-Freudian psychoanalysis for 6 years. Then, in 1953 he abandoned psychoanalysis and in January 1955 started conducting what he referred to as *rational psychotherapy*, perhaps the first formalized system of CBT. In 1962, he renamed his treatment *rational emotive therapy*, and then changed the name again in 1993 to *rational emotive behavior therapy*.

Although Ellis was first to formally introduce cognitive strategies into behavior therapies, a number of other important figures deserve mention for further developing cognitive–behavioral treatments in the 1960s and 1970s, including Aaron Beck (the developer of cognitive therapy), Donald Meichenbaum, Marvin Goldfried, Gerald Davison, and Michael Mahoney (Lazarus, 2001). According to Lazarus (2001), the term *cognitive–behavioral therapy* was first used in 1977 by Cyril Franks, in his overview to that year's *Annual Review of Behavior Therapy* (Franks & Wilson, 1977), which discussed the transition from behavior therapy to CBT. A number of early behavior therapists, such as Rachman and Lazarus, would eventually embrace cognitive strategies, although their mentor Joseph Wolpe was more critical of cognitive approaches throughout his career (e.g., Wolpe, 1997).

Another important evolution in behavioral treatments was recognition of the importance of social learning processes, such as modeling or observational learning. In addition to learning through classical and operant conditioning processes, Stanford University psychologist Albert Bandura recognized that people also learn by observing others. Bandura (1969) and colleagues demonstrated the ways in which social learning can contribute to both adaptive and maladaptive behaviors. Today, modeling is often a component of behavioral treatments, including exposure therapy and social skills training, for example. In addition, Bandura (1986) emphasized the importance of cognition in his theory, which he now refers to as *social-cognitive theory*.

More recently, what is sometimes called a third wave of behavior therapy has emerged (S. C. Hayes, Follette, & Linehan, 2004). In this context, the first wave refers to behavioral treatments that are closely tied to the work of Skinner and Watson, whereas second-wave therapies refer to behavior therapies that incorporate cognitive strategies. Third-wave treatments emphasize the importance of acceptance as a strategy for dealing with unwanted thoughts, emotions, and physical feelings, as well as the importance of living a life that is consistent with what matters to the individual (i.e., the individual's values). Previously, behavioral treatments had generally not explicitly emphasized the importance of attending to a client's personal values.

These approaches (sometimes referred to as *acceptance-based behavior therapies*) often include mindfulness-based practices and other strategies designed to facilitate an acceptance-oriented stance rather than a control-oriented stance. Examples of these acceptance-based behavioral treatments include acceptance and commitment therapy (S. C. Hayes, Strosahl, & Wilson, 1999), mindfulness-based cognitive therapy (Segal, Williams, & Teasdale, 2002), and dialectical behavior therapy (Linehan, 1993a). The popularity of these approaches has increased dramatically in recent years as data supporting their use continue to emerge.

Over the past half century, behavior therapy has evolved from a fledgling model of psychotherapy meeting with considerable resistance to a mainstream treatment approach that is practiced throughout the world. More than 20 scientific journals are now devoted to behavior therapy, and associations devoted to behavior therapies now exist in many different countries (Spiegler & Guevremont, 2010). Although it is not clear how behavior therapies will change in the coming years, behavior therapy will continue to evolve, if history is any indication.

3

Theory

Reviews of behavior therapy often focus more on the techniques than the theory underlying them. However, to conduct behavior therapy skillfully, one must understand the conceptual basis and intention of the specific techniques, beginning with the overarching goals of behavior therapy.

GOALS OF BEHAVIOR THERAPIES

The overarching goal of behavior therapies is to help clients to develop flexible behavioral repertoires that are sensitive to environmental contingencies and are maximally effective for the individual (e.g., Drossel, Rummel, & Fisher, 2009). From a behavioral perspective, a wide range of clinical problems are seen as evidence of habitual, stuck patterns of responding that have developed over time because of associations and contingencies in the environment (which can also include the internal environment, e.g., physical sensations, thoughts, imagery) that maintained these patterns in a given context (described more fully later in this chapter). Therapy is therefore focused on identifying the factors that are currently maintaining the difficulties in question and on intervening to reduce problematic behaviors and responses and increase more flexible, adaptive behaviors and responses. A central focus is on broadening behavioral repertoires and encouraging alternative, adaptive repertoires that will enhance well-being and functioning, rather than on symptom reduction (Drossel, Rummel, & Fisher, 2009). That is, the intent is to help clients to engage in a range of behaviors that are likely to help them function in their lives rather than solely to reduce their anxiety or depressive symptoms.

An initial goal, therefore, is the careful assessment and analysis of presenting problems to determine the contexts in which they occur, the stimuli that trigger their occurrence, and the consequences that maintain them. This functional analysis (described in depth in Chapter 4) helps the client and the therapist to see the ways in which problematic patterns of responding emerge in response to specific cues and are maintained by specific consequences. It also helps to determine whether problematic responses can be understood as resulting from learned associations, reinforcing consequences, or skills deficits, which will have implications for intervention. This analysis also helps to determine how multiple problems interact so that treatment targets can be chosen that will optimize positive outcomes by influencing more than one presenting problem. Although people often think of cues and contingencies as explaining only overt, simplistic behavior problems, such as phobias, these same models can be used to understand more complex patterns of responding, such as those that underlie relationship difficulties. For instance, a client who presents for treatment because of relationship concerns might first be asked to monitor when concerning interactions with a partner occur. Functional analysis may reveal that the client has developed a habit of responding to perceived instances of rejection (which take the behavioral form of the client's partner being focused on something else, or seeming distant) by feeling hurt and vulnerable. The client may habitually respond to these feelings by expressing anger through criticism or storming out of the room, behaviors that are reinforced by the initial reduction in hurt and vulnerability that the client experiences. However, these behaviors increase the partner's tendency to withdraw, thus perpetuating the problematic cycle of interaction. This analysis provides several potential targets for intervention: the client's learned emotional response to the partner's behavior and the client's behavioral responses to feeling hurt and vulnerable. If the couple were in treatment together, a functional analysis of the partner's behavior would also be conducted, providing additional targets for intervention.

In behavior therapy, the therapist and client collaboratively set specific treatment goals and the therapist shares with the client the model of how these goals will be met. Therapy is active in that the client engages in exercises both within and between sessions designed to develop and strengthen new learning and new patterns of responding and to weaken old, habitual ways of responding. Given the emphasis on new learning, practice is an essential part of treatment, requiring the client to actively engage with the treatment. *Actively engaging* means that it is essential that the client agree with the rationale for and goals of treatment. Therapists need to be sensitive to indications that the conceptualization and plan make sense to the client. As in all treatments, the therapist should be attuned to and familiar with both general cultural views that may affect how a client views health, clinical problems, and goals for treatment and the specific perspective of a client and his or her family. These perspectives should all shape the developing conceptualization and plan.

Behavior therapy is flexible and iterative. Therapists and clients are continually evaluating the impact of interventions and the continued relevance of stated goals. Alterations are made to treatment plans on the basis of the effects of interventions, the feasibility of specific interventions for a given individual, and changing external circumstances. The scientific basis of behavior therapy makes continual hypothesis testing an explicit characteristic of this approach to treatment. The findings from a functional analysis are always treated as a working hypothesis, and ongoing assessment and reflection are used to reevaluate and revise these models and intervention plans in order to promote optimal functioning for the individual.

Thus, the goals of behavior therapy are idiographic and are determined and refined collaboratively in the therapeutic relationship. An overarching goal of flexible, adaptive functioning is consistent across clients and presenting problems, but the specifics of what this will look like for a given individual depend on the context and what is most important to the client. Behavior therapists are careful not to assume that they know what is optimal functioning for an individual, but instead aim to help the individual examine his or her life to determine what will be optimal for her or him.

KEY CONCEPTS IN BEHAVIOR THERAPIES

As noted in the preceding chapter, behavior therapy is a broad category that encompasses a wide range of intervention strategies, as well as variability in theoretical emphases. Behavior therapists incorporate various behavioral approaches (e.g., cognitive, mindfulness based) to differing degrees. Also, because behavior therapists emphasize the importance of scientific inquiry, theories that underlie these approaches are constantly being refined on the basis of scientific study and discovery. However, several shared theoretical assumptions characterize therapy based in the behavioral tradition. In this chapter, we provide an overview of these theoretical assumptions and also discuss some of the points of disparity among behavior therapists.

Theory plays an important role in behavior therapies that is often overlooked. The importance that behaviorists (and cognitive behaviorists) place on empirical study has led to the development of numerous manualized treatments that can be subjected to careful, controlled evaluation to examine the efficacy of a specific approach. Although this approach has many advantages, one disadvantage is that it can give the impression that behavior therapy is a collection of techniques rather than a coherent way of understanding human behavior and optimizing human functioning. An emphasis on technique can leave clinicians who are implementing interventions at a loss when aspects of a specific strategy do not fit well with a given client. A clear understanding of the theory underlying specific strategies helps therapists to flexibly implement treatments, responding to individual clients' needs while remaining consistent with the underlying model of the treatment. For instance, strategies can be adjusted so that they are more culturally consistent for a given client while still corresponding to the intervention's initial intent. For example, relaxation imagery that incorporates other people may be more resonant for individuals who identify themselves in relation to others than solitary images that are more commonly used, leading these individuals to practice using imagery more regularly and benefit more from treatment (La Roche, D'Angelo, Gualdron, & Leavell, 2006).

ALL BEHAVIOR SERVES A FUNCTION

A central assumption of behavior therapists is that problematic patterns of behavior happen for a reason. That is, even behaviors that seem to be destructive or clearly harmful to an individual, such as substance dependence, deliberate self-harm, or an abusive relationship, make sense in the context of an individual's learning history. In the context of behavior therapy, the term *behavior* applies to a wide range of client responses, including thoughts, physiological responses, emotional responses, and covert behaviors as well as overt behaviors. Using a behavioral conceptualization, even responses that seem irrational, such as extreme anxiety in response to apparently nonthreatening cues or guilt and shame in response to apparently benign interpersonal exchanges, happen because of biological predispositions and prior learning experiences that have shaped a client to have certain types of responses to particular stimuli. In this way, puzzling behaviors can actually be explained and understood because of previous learning experiences (which we describe in more detail shortly).

Thus, a central goal in behavior therapies is to determine the potential function of presenting problems. This determination serves several purposes in therapy. First, as the therapist and client work together to understand why the client is repeatedly having responses or engaging in behaviors that she or he sees as problematic, these puzzling responses begin to make more sense and seem less baffling. More important, the client often experiences a reduction in self-blame and criticism as a result of this increased understanding of why she or he is responding in this way. For instance, clients with a long-standing history of anxiety often experience relief when the fight-or-flight response, paths to learning fear, and the natural but fear-maintaining response of avoidance are explained to them. Although this understanding alone is often not enough to alter responding, it does often help to reduce the criticism, judgment, and shame that can exacerbate anxious responding and further interfere with relationships and general functioning.

Although the validation that comes with a behavioral conceptualization is likely an active ingredient in behavior therapies, a more important goal is the identification of targets for intervention and strategies that will promote new learning that is more adaptive and growth enhancing. An understanding of principles of learning (described more fully in the next section) is an important foundation in developing intervention strategies that will most efficiently lead to robust new learning.

Behavior Is Learned; New Behavior Can Be Learned Through Early Cue Detection and Practice

Behavior therapies are based on an assumption that individuals have learned to respond and act in the ways they habitually respond and act through identifiable principles of learning. As noted in Chapter 2, behavior therapies evolved from experimental research that detailed these learning principles. Modern behavior therapies are similarly informed by newer developments in experimental research that have identified complexities in principles of learning (e.g., Bouton, Mineka, & Barlow, 2001; Craske et al., 2008). An in-depth discussion of these principles and complexities is beyond the scope of this book (see Bouton, Woods, Moody, Sunshay, & García-Gutiérrez, 2006; Craske & Mystkowski, 2006; O'Donohue & Fisher, 2009), but we provide a summary so that therapists can use these principles to guide implementation of behavior therapies.

Learning Through Association

Both humans and animals learn to associate stimuli that frequently appear together. *Classical conditioning* refers to the process through which a previously neutral stimulus becomes associated with a stimulus that evokes certain responses (either aversive or appetitive). Through being repeatedly paired with an unconditioned stimulus (US) that naturally evokes a given response, the conditioned stimulus (CS) becomes a cue for the US and elicits similar or related responses. This process is clearly evolutionarily adaptive in that organisms learn that the presence of certain stimuli indicates that a threat is likely to appear or that something desirable is likely to appear, and respond accordingly. Once a stimulus has been conditioned, it can lead to new learning by being paired with another previously neutral stimulus, which will in turn come to be associated with the CS and elicit similar or related responses.[1] Through this process of higher order conditioning, more stimuli come to be associated with undesirable or desirable events. Also, through stimulus generalization, stimuli that are similar to the CS also become learned cues, so that eventually a broad range of stimuli are associated and evoke similar responses. For instance, a learned fear of a bright red shirt might lead an individual to respond with anxiety or fear to anything red in the environment.

A client, Monique, can be used to illustrate these principles. Monique presented for therapy reporting that she was anxious and uneasy in social situations. A functional analysis, including monitoring of her symptoms and exploration of specific incidents of anxiety during the previous week, revealed that she responded with physiological arousal and anxious thoughts when she interacted with people who looked or sounded critical. She described her father as extremely critical when she was growing up and stated that he would often turn his attention to other people or walk away after he had criticized her for something. In this example, this withdrawal of attention and affection from a parent was a US that would have naturally elicited fear in a child. Its pairing with criticism from her father led Monique to respond to her father's criticism with anxiety because she

---

[1] Initially, this learning process was thought to involve learning a response to a stimulus because that stimulus had been associated with another stimulus that automatically elicited that response. However, an extensive body of research has demonstrated that an association is learned between the previously neutral stimulus and the US and that associations are also learned regarding the context in which these pairings take place (Rescorla, 1988). In addition, conditioning can result in a different response to the CS than the response to the US, one that is preparatory for the potential occurrence of the US and matched to the properties of the CS (Rescorla, 1988). Although classical conditioning continues to often be described in terms of learning responses, the term *learned associations* is a technically more accurate description of this type of learning.

anticipated the removal of his attention and affection. Gradually, these associations generalized, and she came to have similar responses to any instances of perceived criticism, leading her to feel anxious in a broad range of social situations.

People are particularly prone to learning threatening cues because it is evolutionarily adaptive to identify markers for potential harm and danger so that individuals can avoid this harm or danger. In addition, some individuals are probably biologically predisposed to learn threat more easily and robustly and are therefore more prone to anxiety (e.g., Lonsdorf et al., 2009). Prior experiences with threat, or modeling of fear behavior by significant role models, may also make it more likely that an individual will easily learn to fear cues, and those responses will generalize (Mineka & Zinbarg, 2006). Biology, prior experiences, and modeling likely play a role in other kinds of learning, such as the reinforcing properties of alcohol and drugs (e.g., Enoch, 2007).

Initial models of associative learning identified the conditions under which learned associations (to CSs) could be extinguished such that an organism no longer responded to the CS as though it were associated with the US. Further study has indicated that the term *extinction* is a misnomer because associations are not, in fact, unlearned. Instead, new, competing, nonthreatening associations are learned. So, in the case of fear conditioning, repeated exposure to the CS in the absence of the US will lead to a new, nonthreatening association to the CS, such that fear is no longer the predominant response. Extinction can therefore be thought of as *inhibitory learning* (Craske et al., 2008) in that an association that inhibits the previous association is learned. Rescorla and Wagner (1972) noted that learning is an adjustment that occurs when there is a discrepancy between the outcome that is expected and the outcome that occurs. So extinction trials promote new learning in that the expected association does not occur, so that the CS comes to be associated with "not US" instead of the US.

Bouton et al. (2006) recently reviewed the literature that suggests that conditioned associations, as well as conditions that are likely to make extinction or inhibitory learning more robust, are not unlearned. Animal research has demonstrated that even after extensive extinction of fearful associations, the continued presence of these associations is demonstrated by (a) a renewal effect, in which a learned association to a CS returns when the CS is presented in a different context from the extinction trials; (b) spontaneous recovery, in which a learned association to a CS returns after the passage of time; (c) reinstatement, in which a learned association to a CS returns after the US is presented alone and the CS is presented later; and (d) rapid reacquisition, in which an association to a previously extinguished CS is learned much more rapidly in new conditioning trials. All of these phenomena suggest that a learned fearful association is maintained despite successful extinction. Bouton et al. interpreted these findings as evidence that extinction learning is context specific, which makes sense from an evolutionary standpoint—people learn cues for fear easily, and generalize them, yet learning of inhibitory responses to feared stimuli is more context specific. This serves an important survival function in that individuals will not prematurely learn that a given stimulus is safe simply because it was safe in a specific context. However, it makes it more likely that learned fears will recur, making it important for therapists to address relapse prevention in therapy, so that clients are prepared for these recurrences and are able to continue to approach feared stimuli to promote more robust extinction learned across multiple contexts. Researchers have also suggested that the presence of retrieval cues during extinction trials will help extinction (or inhibitory learning) to generalize to novel contexts (Craske et al., 2008).

Although associative learning is often described in terms of learned associations to external stimuli, there is also extensive evidence that organisms learn associations to internal stimuli as well (for an extensive review of this literature in the context of panic disorder, see Bouton et al., 2001). As a result, people's own internal sensations can become threat cues, leading them to respond with anxiety, which strengthens the cue, potentially leading to a spiral of anxiety or panic. From a behavioral perspective, thoughts can also become associated with a US. As such, thoughts or memories of a traumatic event can elicit posttraumatic responses, even in the absence of the event itself. Thoughts can also have appetitive associations, so that a thought of a drink can lead to a powerful conditioned response of craving for an individual addicted to alcohol. Because these internal cues are beyond people's instrumental control (they cannot avoid thoughts of drinking or anxious sensations completely), these associations are particularly likely to lead to clinical problems. As such, learning new associations to these cues is often an important target of treatment (as is learning not to respond to them behaviorally, as discussed later).

Learning Through Consequences

Behavioral conceptualizations and interventions are also based on the principle that organisms learn through the consequences of their actions. Principles of operant learning suggest that some consequences (i.e., those that are desired) will increase the frequency of a given behavior, or reinforce the behavior, and others (i.e., those that are not desired) will decrease the frequency of a given behavior, or punish the behavior. As such, any frequent behavior is assumed to be reliably associated with a consequence that is desired by the organism, even if there are also apparent consequences that might be assumed to be punishing. For example, a child who finds attention from a teacher to be desirable may continually act out in class because the attention she or he receives after acting out increases the frequency of the behavior, even though the teacher intends this attention to reduce the frequency of the behavior.

Several aspects of operant learning have important implications for understanding difficulties commonly seen in clients. First, immediate consequences generally influence behavior more strongly than do delayed consequences. Again, this makes sense from an evolutionary perspective because a consequence that is more proximal to a given action is more likely to be causally related to the action. However, this often leads to habitual behaviors that have destructive long-term consequences, despite immediately desirable consequences. Substance use is a classic illustration of these principles. Using substances typically has a number of initial consequences that are desirable, such as increased positive affect, decreased distress, and social connection. These are powerful contingencies that can make it very difficult to reduce the frequency of use, despite an individual's awareness of a number of detrimental longer term effects of use (e.g., relational, occupational, and health-related problems). Associative learning also plays a role in substance use in that a wide range of cues come to be strongly associated with use and therefore elicit cravings that are difficult to ignore.

Reinforcers and punishers are defined by their effects on behavior (i.e., whether they increase or decrease the frequency of behavior, respectively). One cannot assume that a given consequence will necessarily act as either a reinforcer or a punisher because the value of a specific consequence is individually determined (and is likely based on learning history). Thus, certain consequences may be reinforcing for a given individual because they have previously been associated with other valued stimuli, but they may be meaningless, or punishing, for another individual. In the example presented earlier, for a child who commonly receives positive attention from adults, the negative attention of being scolded for misbehaving is less likely to be reinforcing and may have the punishing effect intended by the teacher. Certain facial expressions or tones of voice might be reinforcing for one individual who associates them with a loving parent but punishing for another individual whose abusive parent demonstrated similar modes of expression.

One aspect of operant terminology that is often confusing and is commonly misused is the terms *positive* and *negative*. *Positive reinforcement* refers to the presentation of something after a behavior that increases the likelihood that that behavior will recur (e.g., receiving a commission after selling a car is likely to increase sales over time), whereas *negative reinforcement* refers to the removal of something after a behavior that similarly increases the likelihood that that behavior will recur (e.g., a reduction in headache pain after taking medication is likely to increase the use of medication over time in response to headaches). Often, people erroneously use *negative reinforcement* when they mean *punishment*, or a consequence that makes it less likely a given behavior will recur.

Negative reinforcement is frequently a function of clinically relevant behaviors. Individuals often engage in behaviors that reduce or remove their distressing feelings or thoughts, thus negatively reinforcing the behavior and making it more likely they will engage in the behavior again (for an extensive review of experiential avoidance as a common function of clinical problems, see S. C. Hayes, Wilson, Gifford, Follette, & Strosahl, 1996). For instance, a natural behavioral response to threat cues is to escape or avoid them. This behavior is negatively reinforced by the immediate reduction in anxiety that an organism experiences, making it more likely that avoidance will recur. However, this avoidance also maintains fear by interfering with the extinction or inhibitory learning process described earlier. In this way, individuals can continue to experience anxiety in response to cues that are not truly indicators of threat, but have been associated with threat in the past, because their habitual avoidance impedes any new learning of a nonfearful association with the cue. As noted earlier, substance abuse may also be negatively reinforced by initially reducing or removing anxious, depressive, angry, or other distressing emotions, leading individuals to be more likely to drink or use drugs again. In fact, lapses in alcohol use after treatment are significantly associated with increases in negative affect (Witkiewitz & Aracelliz Villarroel, 2009). Similar functions have been proposed for eating-disordered behavior and deliberate self-harm (for a review, see Roemer & Orsillo, 2009).

Findings from experimental research have indicated that broader, flexible behavioral repertoires are more adaptive than narrowed, rigid repertoires (Drossel, Rummel, & Fisher, 2009). Broad, flexible repertoires allow for new learning to occur, so that an organism can function optimally even as contexts change so that consequences for a given behavior are different than they were during previous learning experiences. Clinical problems can be conceptualized as rigid, narrowed behavioral repertoires, and expansion of these repertoires is needed to help the individual engage in behaviors that will be naturally reinforced by his or her environment. For example, Joe learned to withdraw in response to communications of anger, which was adaptive growing up when his mother's anger would escalate to violence. However, with his partner, he now withdraws when he detects even the slightest amount of annoyance, which his partner experiences as rejecting, escalating his negative affective experience and contributing to the cycle of the couple's distress. If Joe can learn to expand his behavioral repertoire so that he can instead communicate directly when he perceives that his partner is annoyed, this new behavior may be reinforced by increased intimacy and cooperation, which would in turn decrease the couple's distress. Thus, the new behavior would be both positively and negatively reinforced, so that it would gradually become more likely over time.

Cues are also relevant to operant learning. A discriminant stimulus that has been associated with a given behavior leading to a specific consequence becomes a cue to exhibit or inhibit the target behavior. In this way, individuals learn to behave in certain ways with a parent or teacher who is likely to reinforce certain behaviors and to refrain from other behaviors with a parent or teacher who is likely to punish them. Patterns of behaving that are insensitive to cues and contexts are particularly likely to be problematic and are often the source of clinical consultation. In the case of Joe, the behaviors he learned with his mother became a generalized pattern, and he failed to respond specifically to the cues present with his partner that indicated that a different behavior would be adaptive.

In working with Joe, the goal of treatment was to help him develop new behaviors that were sensitive to the novel discriminant stimulus of his partner. With other clients, the goal is to reduce the connection between the stimulus and the behavior. For example, many behaviors with an experiential avoidant function are cued by internal stimuli such as arousal, anxious thoughts, or negative affect. Over time, the individual learns to consistently respond to these cues with these behaviors, which are often followed immediately by at least slight decreases in distress, which further reinforce the behaviors. However, these behaviors can cause more long-term difficulties, including maintaining conditioned anxiety, as described earlier. Thus, treatment may focus on exposure to the cues (both internal and external) and prevention of the learned response, or response prevention. For instance, Jamila reported recurrent obsessive thoughts about germs causing disease in her family and habitually responded to these thoughts by cleaning compulsively. In therapy, she gradually learned to notice these thoughts and her urge to clean, but to refrain from cleaning in response to them. Over time, although she still had the thoughts from time to time, they were not as closely tied to the urge to clean, and she was able to engage in other aspects of her life more fully.

Early cue detection is an important element of new learning. As habitual patterns of responding are identified, the therapist and client use monitoring and review of the previous week to identify early cues for these behavioral patterns. When patterns of responding are identified earlier and earlier in the cycle, it becomes easier to practice alternative behaviors and responses and to develop new patterns of responding. For example, if a client notices the moment that he experiences tension in his shoulders, it is much easier to implement a relaxation strategy in that moment than if he waits until his anxious thoughts and reactions have begun to spiral into a much higher level of anxiety. New responses can be practiced at any point in the cycle, but earlier application is more likely to lead to desirable consequences, thus reinforcing the new behavior.

Behavior therapists typically emphasize reinforcement strategies as opposed to punishment strategies for a number of reasons (Drossel, Rummel, & Fisher, 2009). First, punishment is commonly associated with negative emotional responses, which can come to be associated with the person providing the punishment. As such, punishment may have a negative effect on the therapeutic relationship. Also, punishment only reduces the frequency of a behavior; it does not promote an alternative, adaptive behavior. Thus, punishment further narrows behavioral repertoires rather than expanding them. Each behavior occurs in a given context because its association to reinforcers is stronger than its association to punishers and because the association of alternative behaviors to reinforcers is less strong. Strengthening the reinforcing associations of an alternative, incompatible behavior will therefore also decrease the likelihood of the target behavior without introducing the less desirable correlates of punishment.

As noted earlier, the nature of the reinforcers that will be influential is specific to individuals and may also be specific to given contexts. A careful functional analysis is necessary to determine the consequences that are likely to increase the frequency of a desired behavior. Natural reinforcers will be more powerful than artificial or contrived reinforcers because they are more likely to occur in the client's environment and will therefore help maintain the new behavior outside of therapy. Social reinforcers—or attention, acknowledgment, praise, and approval from other people—are particularly powerful forms of reinforcement because people naturally seek these consequences and they occur naturally in people's environments (Spiegler & Guevremont, 2010). However, Kohlenberg and Tsai (1995) provided a useful clinical example of how social reinforcers in therapy can also be contrived or artificial. When working with a client who has difficulty expressing his anger, a therapist might be inclined to respond to an expression of anger by smiling and saying, "I'm so glad you shared those feelings with me." However, it is very unlikely that anyone in the client's life will respond similarly to this kind of communication. However, if the therapist attends to the source of the client's anger and makes an attempt to address it accordingly, this more natural contingency might also be maintained in the client's life.

Therapy can be used to increase the reinforcing value of behaviors when the positive consequences of these behaviors are more long term and therefore do not automatically influence behaviors. From a behavioral perspective, this alteration of the reinforcement value of behaviors is a way of enhancing motivation (Drossel, Rummel, & Fisher, 2009). For instance, motivational interviewing (Miller & Rollnick, 2002) helps the client to identify the ways in which current behaviors are inconsistent with longer term goals or values. This process will likely serve to decrease the reinforcing properties of goal-inconsistent behaviors (e.g., avoiding social interactions or drinking excessively) while increasing the reinforcing properties of goal-consistent behaviors (e.g., initiating social contact or choosing not to take a drink). Similarly, values clarification, an element of acceptance and commitment therapy and other acceptance-based behavior therapies (e.g., K. G. Wilson & Murrell, 2004), helps clients to identify what is personally meaningful to them (e.g., being responsive to a family member or pursuing work that is intellectually challenging). This connection to meaning can enhance the reinforcing properties of behaviors that are otherwise not as strongly immediately reinforcing (e.g., sitting down to write) while refraining from behaviors that are more readily reinforced but less valued by the individual.

Interestingly, people's own behavior can serve as a reinforcer for other behaviors. The *Premack principle* refers to the consistent finding that high-frequency behaviors that occur reliably after the occurrence of low-frequency behaviors will increase the frequency of those low-frequency behaviors

(Premack, 1965). For example, if while writing this book we found that sitting down to write had become a low-frequency behavior and checking e-mail was a high-frequency behavior, if we intentionally only check e-mail after having written for 60 minutes, checking e-mail would reinforce our writing behavior and we would begin to sit down to write more frequently. Spiegler and Guevremont (2010) presented a case example of a psychiatric patient who was not engaging in any social behaviors and whose only frequent behavior was sitting in a chair. When the hospital staff introduced contingencies so that she could sit in the chair only after engaging in some sort of social interaction and gradually increased the length of social interaction required for the chair sitting to occur (beginning with 2 minutes), within 3 weeks the patient was spending more time socializing than sitting in the chair.

Different schedules of reinforcement yield different patterns of responding. Continuous reinforcement, or reinforcing a behavior each time it occurs, is most helpful when a new behavior is being learned. However, once a behavior is established, an intermittent reinforcement schedule, or only reinforcing a behavior some of the times it occurs, leads to more robust behavior that is more likely to continue over time and in multiple contexts. An intermittent schedule is similar to the reinforcement that occurs naturally in people's lives. Often, the persistence of a problematic behavior can be understood by past experiences of intermittent reinforcement. For instance, people often have a difficult time ending relationships that are occasionally extremely positive (and thus powerfully reinforcing) despite extended times when they are negative (and thus not reinforcing at all). This phenomenon may help explain people remaining in abusive relationships— the "honeymoon period" after an abusive outburst is often powerfully reinforcing, leading the victim to stay in the relationship.

An individual's ability to exhibit a given behavior is also an important consideration in trying to expand a client's behavioral repertoire. Often, the learning histories that have narrowed behavioral repertoires have also failed to promote learning of important skills, such as emotional awareness and regulation (cf. Linehan, 1993a) or social skills. These skills deficits may further impede new learning because it is difficult for the client to act in a way that is naturally reinforced by her or his environment. In these cases, instruction in skills can be an important part of therapy (as described in Chapter 4). However, humans naturally respond to subtle discriminative stimuli in social situations that cannot be captured in instruction (Drossel, Garrison-Diehn, & Fisher, 2009), so behavioral learning remains an important aspect of skills training. In addition, natural reinforcers for performing the skills (e.g., expressions of understanding when a client describes an emotional experience) will be more powerful than artificial reinforcers (e.g., verbal praise), although artificial reinforcers may initially be useful for establishing the newly learned behavior.

Learning Through Observation

Early behavior theory focused on direct experience as a central source for learning. However, Bandura (1977b) noted that individuals can learn vicariously as well as from direct experience. A wealth of research has documented that both associative and operant learning can also happen through observation. A classic set of studies demonstrated that even monkeys can learn to associate fear with a stimulus (in this case, a snake when a lab-reared monkey had no prior experience with snakes) by observing another monkey respond to this stimulus with fear (M. Cook, Mineka, Wolkenstein, & Laitsch, 1985). The monkeys could also be inoculated against the fear learning if they observed a monkey responding nonfearfully to a snake before their exposure to the fearful model, suggesting that modeling can also inoculate against fear learning (Mineka & Cook, 1986). These findings (and consistent findings in the human literature) indicated that individuals may learn to fear specific contexts and cues because of modeling from their parents or other influential people in their lives, and they may also learn not to fear cues and contexts if people in their lives model approach behavior toward potentially threatening cues and contexts.

Bandura's classic Bobo doll studies revealed that operant learning can be observational as well. In one study (Bandura, 1965), children watched a film in which a model behaved aggressively toward a Bobo doll and was reinforced or punished or no contingency was presented. In a subsequent free-play period, children were more likely to imitate the aggressive behavior if they had observed the model being reinforced and were less likely to do so if they had observed the model being punished for the behavior.

These findings are often considered evidence that witnessing aggressive behavior may lead to aggressive behavior for some individuals. More broadly, an individual's ability to learn from watching other people leads to these people potentially having a significant influence on the behavioral patterns developed by the individual. Observational learning also explains one mechanism for socialization influences because media influences provide models of behavior that will be reinforced, behavior that will be punished, and characteristics that are associated with having more control over reinforcers in society.

Verbal Learning

Although many behavioral principles can be studied in both animals and humans, language is clearly an important aspect of human experience, and its role in learning also needs to be addressed. Humans can learn about associations and consequences by simply having them described by someone they trust. This rule-governed learning can lead individuals to exhibit behaviors they might not have engaged in on their own and also to refrain from exhibiting other behaviors, without ever experiencing any contingency-based learning. Although this ability to learn from instruction is clearly adaptive—one can learn not to cross the street without looking both ways without ever experiencing the consequence of being hit by a car or witnessing someone else being hit by a car—it also presents some potential challenges.

Rule-governed learning is particularly likely to be insensitive to contingencies so that one can continue to be guided by beliefs about contingencies when one has not experienced those contingencies and, in fact, the contingencies may be inaccurate (for a review of this research, see S. C. Hayes, Strosahl, & Wilson, 1999). If these rules have taught an individual not to exhibit certain behaviors, the person may never have the direct experience of how satisfying these behaviors might be. Often, a target of therapy is helping clients to recognize that they are behaving in ways that they were taught but that do not match their own experience of contingencies. For instance, when he was growing up, Dominic's parents explicitly taught him that emotional vulnerability would be punished by other people and should be avoided. As a result, he developed a pattern of concealing his emotional distress from people in his life. He was reinforced for his "emotional strength" through praise and increased affection from his parents any time something upsetting happened and he did not communicate an emotional reaction to it. In adulthood, Dominic struggled to develop close interpersonal relationships, and his partners and friends often said they found him to be distant or unaffected in a way that made them feel less close to him. In therapy, Dominic expressed a strong desire for emotional intimacy and was puzzled by other people's responses to him. However, when he began to identify his patterns of responding during times of distress, he was able to see that he repeatedly had thoughts such as "People don't like to be around people who are an emotional wreck" or "No one wants to see me break down." These were rules his parents had taught him, and they were continuing to guide his behavior, even when people around him were clearly indicating that they might no longer apply. As he became more aware of this, he was able to try out new behaviors, such as sharing his emotional responses with people in his life. These new behaviors were reinforced by increased intimacy, which helped him further develop and solidify these new, more adaptive behavioral patterns.

Although rule-governed behavior can be problematic because it can become rigid and nonresponsive to changing contingencies, verbal instruction can play a useful role in changing patterns of responding and establishing new, more flexible patterns. In therapy, clients and therapists may come up with hypotheses regarding behavior changes that might be more adaptive and satisfying for the individual. This verbally derived hypothesis can help the client to implement new behaviors or refrain from habitual behavioral responses to specific cues. To be maintained and to be adaptively flexible, such changes will eventually need to be reinforced by the environment, but verbal instruction can be very beneficial in initiating behavior change.

Role of Learning History

Although the focus of functional analysis is on current, maintaining factors of behaviors, history of reinforcement also plays an important role in understanding current clinical problems. For example, extensive animal and human research has demonstrated the role that a history of non-reinforcement for instrumental behaviors can play in current inaction. In a classic study, dogs were exposed to inescapable shocks; when they pressed a lever, the shocks they were receiving did not terminate. When they were placed in a new situation in which they could escape and avoid the shock, they instead laid down and whined, having learned that their actions did not control the occurrence of the shock (Overmier & Seligman, 1967). This learned helplessness provides a useful model for explaining depressive symptoms. Individuals who have historically experienced minimal positive or negative reinforcement for their behaviors may learn not to engage in instrumental behaviors, becoming behaviorally inactive and perpetuating depressive symptoms by reducing any contact with potential reinforcers. Behavioral activation (described in Chapter 4) is a treatment that targets this learned inaction by promoting increased action and increasing contact with behavioral reinforcers. This model is also useful in understanding the potential psychological consequences of identifying with a marginalized group and chronically experiencing a lack of control over reinforcers as a result of systemic oppression.

An extensive body of research has also demonstrated that prior learning history plays an important role in the development of anxiety disorders (for a review, see Mineka & Zinbarg, 2006). For example, previous exposure to a potential CS in the absence of any US can inoculate against the development of fears. Studies have found that children who have had many nontraumatic experiences with dentists are less likely to develop dental anxiety after a negative event with a dentist than children with fewer prior nontraumatic experiences (Kent, 1997). This finding is consistent with those of the observational learning study described earlier in which monkeys were inoculated against developing fear of a snake by prior exposure to a nonfearful model (Mineka & Cook, 1986). In addition, a history of mastery or control over reinforcers can serve to inoculate against the development of fearful associations. In a classic study, Mineka, Gunnar, and Champoux (1986) found that monkeys who had been raised for months with control over food and water demonstrated less fear and more exploratory behavior than those who were not given control over these reinforcers.

Role of Cognition in Behavior Therapy

The role of cognition has been, and continues to be, a topic of significant discussion among behavior therapists. Initially, as reviewed in Chapter 2, behavior theory focused primarily on animal models of human behavior and emphasized stimuli, responses, and consequences in understanding clinical problems. As models of learning developed and expanded, more attention was paid to cognitive constructs such as attention and memory. Theorists such as Bandura noted that individuals developed expectancies about the contingencies that would be present in a given situation, as well as more generally, and that these expectancies also played a role in learning. Clinical problems could then be understood in part as resulting from the development of particular expectancies that would limit the generation of adaptive behaviors. Theorists also noted that the meaning of both cues and consequences, or their stimulus value, played an important role in understanding their effect on individuals' behavior.

Learned expectancies (based on prior direct experience, modeling, and verbal instruction) often play a significant role in behavioral models. Learned expectancies include expectancies regarding the external environment (e.g., how others will respond to specific interpersonal behaviors, or the effect that an individual expects to have on her or his environment), as well as expectancies regarding the individual's ability to respond effectively to environmental circumstances. Bandura's (1977a) self-efficacy theory suggests that an individual's behavior will be guided by expectancies regarding his or her ability to engage in certain tasks (competence), as well as the consequences for these behaviors. Thus, individuals learn to expect that they can be effective in their environments or that they cannot, and this expectancy shapes their future actions. According to Bandura, direct experiences will have the most powerful influence on self-efficacy, although modeling and social persuasion will also influence an individual's self-efficacy. Many behavioral strategies (e.g., exposure-based treatments, behavioral activation) can be understood, then, as increasing a client's self-efficacy by encouraging experiences that demonstrate his or her ability to engage in behaviors that are reinforced by environmental contingencies.

As reviewed in Chapter 2, many behavior therapists have expanded their models to those included under the broad term *cognitive–behavioral therapy*, described in depth by Craske (2010). Under this broad umbrella, therapists subscribe to a range of views regarding the role of cognition. From a traditional behavioral perspective, thoughts are part of a functional analysis, but they are not privileged above any other component (e.g., actions or feelings; Drossel, Rummel, & Fisher, 2009). In other words, thoughts are not seen as necessarily causal but instead serve a function just like any other behavior might. Behavioral theories of verbal learning have recently been further developed through relational frame theory (S. C. Hayes, Barnes-Holmes, & Roche, 2001), which describes the ways in which humans learn bidirectional relationships such that internal stimuli such as thoughts and images can come to serve the same function as the events that they represent. In this way, the thought "I am unlovable and will end up alone" can elicit the same responses as the experience of rejection and social isolation and can affect behavior in a similar way.

Information processing theories also developed under the rubric of cognitive– behavioral theory. These models expand on traditional stimulus, response, and consequence models by incorporating research on attention, encoding, and retrieval, as well as incorporating meaning elements as important aspects of learning. For example, information processing models of anxiety have noted the role that attentional biases toward threat cues and interpretive biases toward perceiving ambiguous situations as threatening heighten the frequency of threat encountered by anxious individuals, further strengthening their anxious responding and interfering with the possibility of learning new, nonthreatening information (for a review, see McNally & Reese, 2008).

Foa and Kozak's (1986) emotional processing theory is a particularly influential information processing model in the behavioral treatment of anxiety disorders. Foa and Kozak drew from information processing research and theory and expanded stimulus response conceptualizations of fear learning by proposing that fearful associations occur in a fear network of stimulus, response, and meaning elements (e.g., "I'm going to die," "I can't tolerate this feeling"). According to this model, conditioning experiences lead these elements to be associated with one another, such that experiencing one makes it likely that the other will occur. Avoidance interferes with new learning so that fear-related elements of the network remain intense and closely connected, without any competing nonfearful association to modulate responding. According to this model, successful treatment involves full activation of the fear network and incorporation of new, corrective information. This emotional processing will lead to alterations in the fear network so that elements become associated with nonthreatening responses and meanings, reducing fearful responding. Foa and Kozak suggested that indicators of successful exposure will be (a) an initial response of fear (indicating activation of the fear network) and (b) reductions in fearful responding both in sessions and across sessions (indicating incorporation of corrective information). However, a recent update of the theory noted that reductions in fearful responding in sessions might not, in fact, be necessary for new information to be incorporated (Foa, Huppert, & Cahill, 2006). In their extensive review of studies of exposure, Craske et al. (2008) noted that the data are not always consistent with these proposed indicators of successful exposure. These authors suggested that exposure-based treatments are effective instead because they provide an opportunity for inhibitory learning (through the development of competing, non-threat-related associations) and the development of tolerance for fear and anxiety.

Other cognitive–behavioral theories evolved to conceptualize thoughts as playing a causal role in clinical problems. According to these models (e.g., Beck, 1976), events cue certain beliefs or automatic thoughts (often based on distorted styles of thinking, e.g., overgeneralization or dichotomous thinking), which result in emotional and behavioral consequences. These beliefs and automatic thoughts are seen as stemming from individuals' schemas, which include assumptions and expectancies that influence mood and behavior by guiding the way information is perceived, encoded, and recalled (Beck, 1993). These cognitive theories emphasize the importance of increasing awareness of these automatic thoughts, identifying the distortions they represent, and challenging them, in order to alter the consequences that follow. Therapists from these traditions engage in a wide range of clinical strategies (described briefly in Chapter 4 and more in depth in Craske, 2010) that vary in terms of how actively they focus on changing cognition versus recognizing cognitions and responding more flexibly to them.

A more recent development in behavior therapy has been an explicit emphasis on acceptance of thoughts, as opposed to efforts to challenge or change thoughts (for a review, see Herbert, Forman, & Englund, 2009). These acceptance-based behavior therapies stem from a range of theoretical backgrounds but share a perspective on cognition in which the source of difficulty is seen as the nature of an individual's relationship to her or his thoughts, not necessarily the content of the thoughts themselves (e.g., S. C. Hayes, Strosahl, & Wilson, 1999; Segal et al., 2002). Put another way, these therapies focus on "changing the antecedent function of rules related to thoughts and feelings" (Drossel, Rummel, & Fisher, 2009, p. 35) rather than changing their frequency. As such, these approaches are congruent with the traditional behavioral view of thoughts as covert behaviors that can serve an important function in maintaining clinically relevant behaviors but are not privileged as causal factors above other behaviors.

Commonalities in Approach to Cognition

Although there is a great deal of debate in the field regarding the most precise and effective way to conceptualize and address cognitions in therapy, important commonalities in the approach to cognitions, even across disparate perspectives within behavior therapies, have also emerged (e.g., Arch & Craske, 2008). Teasdale et al. (2002) found that both traditional cognitive therapy and mindfulness-based cognitive therapy were associated with increases in meta-cognitive awareness, or decentering (recognizing thoughts as mental events rather than as indicators of truth or the nature of the self), which accounted for reductions in risk of depressive relapse. It may be, then, that both the process of identifying and challenging thoughts and the process of enhancing awareness and acceptance of thoughts are effective through the mechanism of altering the antecedent function of thoughts (in other words, changing the responses individuals have to these thoughts and the behaviors they engage in after the thoughts). For example, Sumi came to therapy because she felt socially isolated and lonely. Through monitoring, she discovered that when opportunities to socialize emerged, she immediately had the thought that she would not be able to easily relate to people and as a result they would not like her. After these thoughts, she typically chose to turn down the opportunity to socialize. Over time, she became able to notice these thoughts, as well as her impulse to decline social invitations that often occurred in association with these thoughts. She began to choose instead to engage socially, despite her discomfort and fear. She was able to make this change by cultivating acceptance of her internal experience rather than trying to change these thoughts. However, the same outcome might have occurred if therapy had involved challenging this cognition and generating alternative cognitions that were equally or more likely, which could similarly have led her to be more decentered from the thought and able to engage in actions that were important to her regardless of her thoughts.

Another commonality in the approach to cognition across behavior therapies is an emphasis on the importance of experiential learning. In traditional cognitive therapy, behavioral experiments play an important role in the process of challenging cognitions and developing new, alternative cognitions. In behavioral approaches, although verbal instruction may be used, direct experience is seen as the most powerful and flexible form of learning because it puts individuals in touch with natural contingencies that will maintain behavior change and allow for flexible responding to changing contexts. Experience is also emphasized in cognitive therapy in its emphasis on *hot* cognition, or cognitions that are closely tied to emotional reactions, as opposed to *cold* cognitions, or a more detached mode of thinking. This emphasis on thoughts that are associated with emotional responses makes emotional exposure a significant aspect of even strictly cognitive therapies (Arch & Craske, 2008). As such, all of these approaches likely include a component of learning to tolerate emotional responding or learning new, nonthreatening associations to internal responses that have been associated with threat.

CONCLUSION

This overview of behavior theories was intended to provide a framework for clinical decision making based in empirically supported principles of learning. We have also provided a brief discussion of the varying views of the role of cognition in behavior therapies while identifying some potentially common mechanisms of change among these disparate approaches. In the next chapter, we provide an overview of the strategies that commonly stem from these theories. As described earlier, these strategies should be implemented in accordance with the individualized, culturally sensitive case conceptualization that is derived from a careful functional analysis (as described in the beginning of the next chapter).

4

The Therapy Process

We begin this chapter with a detailed discussion of behavioral assessment and how behavior therapists view the relationship between assessment and treatment. Next, we review specific techniques and strategies that are frequently used by behavior therapists. We also discuss the role of the therapist–client relationship in behavior therapy, along with obstacles and challenges in the use of behavior therapy. Finally, we offer three case examples to illustrate how behavioral techniques are used in practice.

BEHAVIORAL ASSESSMENT

Behavior therapy depends on thorough assessment, typically based on the same behavioral principles that underlie treatment. This section includes a description of the process of behavioral assessment, a discussion of functional assessment (an important aspect of behavioral assessment), and information on some of the most commonly used behavioral assessment techniques.

Description of Behavioral Assessment

As with other forms of psychological assessment, behavioral assessment involves the systematic evaluation of behavior, including motor, cognitive, verbal, and psychophysiological responses. Behavioral assessment grew out of early work in classical and operant conditioning, although it was not commonly used until after the publication of several seminal articles in the 1960s and 1970s, well after behavior therapy had been established (Ollendick, Alvarez, & Greene, 2004). Just as behavioral treatments have become more diverse over time (see Chapter 2), so have the range of assessment techniques used by behavior therapists. Contemporary behavioral assessment still includes traditional methods of assessing behavior, such as behavioral observation, self-monitoring, and functional analysis, but other methods are increasingly being used as well, including self-report scales, cognitive measures, and diagnostic interviews, all of which would not likely have been included in a standard behavioral assessment several decades ago.

Contemporary behavioral assessment has a number of goals, including developing a better understanding of a client's problems (from a behavioral perspective); describing the presence, absence, or severity of particular symptoms; making inferences about the causes of a client's problems (especially environmental influences); predicting future behavior; developing appropriate treatments; and measuring treatment outcome. In the remainder of this section, we highlight some of the most important features of behavioral assessment, with an emphasis on how behavioral assessment differs from other forms of assessment. Detailed reviews of behavioral assessment may be found elsewhere (e.g., Haynes & Heiby, 2004).

Functionalism and Behavioral Assessment

Behavioral assessment emphasizes a functional approach to understanding behavior. In other words, a goal of behavioral assessment is to specify the function or purpose of clients' behaviors (i.e., why people behave the way they do). In practice, this process includes identifying factors that maintain behavior, including environmental triggers, contexts in which behavior occurs, and ways in which behaviors are reinforced or punished by the client's environment. Despite the emphasis on function, behavioral assessment often includes measurement of the structure or form of behavior as well, such as the frequency and severity of specific symptoms and behaviors. Measuring the form that behaviors take is important for assessing the outcome of behavioral treatment because the goal of treatment is often to change the frequency or severity of particular symptoms or behaviors.

Hypothesized Causes of Behavior

In behavioral assessment, causes of behavior are assumed to be based in the client's environment or to stem from interactions among various biological and environmental factors. As such, behavior is expected to vary considerably over time and across situations, as a function of environmental contingencies. For example, a child might scream and cry around a parent who is quick to give in to the child's tantrums but not with another parent who routinely ignores these behaviors. In contrast to behavioral assessment, traditional personality assessment views behavior as stemming from enduring personality traits that are somewhat consistent across time and context. Although some variability across situations might be expected in traditional assessment, the importance of such variability is often minimized, whereas in behavioral assessment the variability in behavior across situations is of primary interest.

Levels of Inference

In behavioral assessment, behavior is assessed directly using observation in the natural environment, as well as other methods. Behaviors are generally taken at face value and are measured directly in situations of interest. Few inferences are made about the meaning of specific behaviors, and personality constructs are rarely discussed in any depth. Rather, personality is assumed to be no more than a shorthand way to describe groups of behaviors. In contrast, projective personality assessments, such as the Rorschach inkblot test, use a high level of inference and interpretation (Exner, 1993) and have been the subject of much criticism for their relative lack of validity (e.g., Wood, Nezworski, Lilienfeld, & Garb, 2003).

Reliance on Idiographic Versus Nomothetic Approaches

The term *idiographic* is derived from the Greek word *idios*, which means "pertaining to one's self." Traditionally, behavioral assessment is an idiographic approach in that the clinician is interested in behavior at the individual level. Each person is viewed as unique, and the goal of assessment is to better understand variability in behavior in the individual. In other words, the clinician attempts to learn why a person's behavior varies over time and across situations. The idiographic approaches differ from nomothetic approaches to assessment, which attempt to understand clients in comparison with some larger group. Nomothetic approaches to assessment include diagnostic assessment, such as structured interviews based on the *Diagnostic and Statistical Manual of Mental Disorders* (4th ed., text rev. [*DSM–IV–TR*]; American Psychiatric Association, 2000), as well as standard psychometric tests, such as the Wechsler Adult Intelligence Scale—IV (Wechsler, 2008) and the Minnesota Multiphasic Personality Inventory—2 (Butcher et al., 2001). In nomothetic approaches, variability within an individual is seen as error or noise (i.e., something to be reduced, minimized, or ignored). In contrast, behavior therapists see variability as something to be explained or understood.

Historically, behavioral assessment has not been used to diagnose clients or to make inferences about how clients compare with normative groups on particular latent variables. That is not to say that in practice behavior therapists do not use nomothetic assessment methods. In fact, many behavior therapists do assign *DSM–IV–TR* diagnoses and may use standard nomothetic measures of personality or intelligence in their practices, in addition to more traditional behavioral assessment methods.

Scope and Timing of Assessments

Behavioral assessment is multimodal. In other words, data are collected from multiple informants (e.g., clients, family members, teachers, friends) when possible and using multiple methods (e.g., interviews, direct observation, diaries, checklists, psychophysiological measures). Behavioral assessment is also ongoing. In other approaches, assessment often occurs before treatment begins (e.g., to establish a diagnosis or measure pretreatment severity of the problem) and occasionally after treatment has ended (e.g., to measure outcome). In behavioral assessment, measures are obtained throughout treatment. For example, a client with panic disorder might be expected to record each panic attack that occurs throughout treatment (including the severity of the attack, the situation in which the attack occurs, and various other features). Data from the assessment are used to evaluate progress on an ongoing basis, to test hypotheses regarding the function of problem behaviors, to inform occasional changes in the direction of treatment, and to assess the short- and long-term effects of particular interventions.

Emphasis on Empiricism

Behavioral assessment assumes that potential threats to reliability and validity are inherent in the assessment process. For example, behaviorally trained clinicians are taught to recognize that selection of target behaviors is likely to be influenced by biases held by both the therapist and the client and that there may be disagreements regarding which target behaviors are most important to focus on during treatment. Using multiple informants, assessment methods, and instruments helps to reduce some of the most common threats to validity in the assessment process. It is also important for assessment to occur on multiple occasions and in a variety of contexts and situations. For example, a socially anxious client may show signs of extreme anxiety during a clinical interview, but it would be a mistake to assume that the client is always anxious on the basis of his or her behavior during a single interview. Rather, it would be important to assess anxiety across a wide range of social situations and other contexts. In addition, the fact that behavioral assessment emphasizes direct and objective measures (e.g., counting panic attacks) helps to reduce certain threats to validity (e.g., interpretational bias) that can otherwise be a problem.

Ideally, clinicians who use behavioral assessment strategies should be familiar with the empirical literature on the measures being used, the problems being assessed, and the factors that are likely to influence their judgment. From a behavioral perspective, clinical judgments should be regarded as hypotheses and should be modifiable, pending new information. When possible, clinicians should conduct experiments to test the validity of their hypotheses. For example, if a therapist suspects that a client's depression is secondary to conflict in her marriage, it might be useful to have the client monitor her mood as well as the occurrence of arguments with her partner over the course of a few weeks to examine the relationship between these two variables.

Functional Assessment

Functional assessment is the process of identifying variables believed to be responsible for maintaining problem behaviors (note that the term *functional assessment* has different meanings in other clinical contexts, such as in neuropsychological assessment, where it refers to the assessment of cognitive or motor functioning). Kenny, Alvarez, Donohue, and Winick (2008) described three main stages in the process of functional assessment. The first step is to identify behaviors that will be targeted in treatment, as well as events that precede (antecedents) and follow (consequences) these behaviors. The second step is functional analysis, which involves developing a behavioral case formulation, in part by manipulating environmental events to measure the effects on target behaviors. The third stage in functional assessment is the development of specific treatment interventions based on the results of the functional assessment. We now discuss each of these stages in turn.

Selection of Target Behaviors

Generally, the client and clinician collaborate on the selection of target behaviors. The process often begins with a broad assessment of potential problem behaviors, using a clinical interview, various self-report questionnaires, and other methods. Data collected from the broad assessment are then reviewed, and potential target behaviors are identified. Target behaviors are typically considered in the context of three behavioral response modes (O'Brien, Kaplar, & Haynes, 2005): (a) *verbal–cognitive* (e.g., thoughts, self-statements, images), (b) *physiological–affective* (e.g., physical sensations, physiological responses, emotional responses), and (c) *overt–motor* (e.g., observable behavioral responses).

When selecting target behaviors, it is important to operationally define and describe the behaviors of interest, including their form, the settings and contexts in which they occur, and their typical frequency, duration, and intensity. Target behaviors are generally those that are most disturbing or dangerous to the client or others, that are amenable to modification, and for which change is most likely to lead to changes in other problem behaviors. Behavior change should be presented to the client in positive terms, with an emphasis on increasing desirable behaviors, rather than eliminating unwanted behaviors, where possible. Ideally, the selection of target behaviors should take into account the likelihood that new behaviors will be reinforced by the client's environment once treatment has ended. Otherwise, the client will be at risk for having the problem behaviors return.

Functional Analysis

Functional analysis is the process of developing a behavioral case formulation that describes the relationships between behavioral antecedents, target behaviors, and consequences. One popular model for summarizing this process is the SORC model, in which S = antecedent *stimuli,* O = factors inherent in the *organism,* R = target *response,* and C = *consequences* (Goldfried & Sprafkin, 1976). In conducting a functional analysis, the clinician should attempt to identify causal relationships among these variables. Some strategies for determining whether a relationship is causal include examining whether (a) the variables are correlated (e.g., does the client tend to drink more alcohol when feeling depressed?), although correlation alone is not enough to assume causation; (b) there is a temporal relationship between the variables (e.g., does the client's depression typically precede or follow the drinking?); (c) there is an explanation for the relationship that makes sense in light of empirical research and theory (e.g., research that speaks to a relationship between alcohol abuse and depression more generally); and (d) alternative explanations have been ruled out (O'Brien et al., 2005).

Kenny et al. (2008) distinguished among three different levels of functional analysis: indirect, descriptive, and experimental. *Indirect functional analysis* involves using information from interviews, questionnaires, and other sources to formulate hypotheses regarding the causal relationships among target behaviors, antecedents, and consequences. For example, a therapist treating a woman with depression might ask the client and her partner whether they are aware of any environmental triggers for the client's low mood (e.g., relationship stress, time of day, spending time with certain people, fatigue, long hours at work, lack of exercise, lack of sleep). *Descriptive functional analysis* involves systematically observing a target behavior to directly assess its relationship with antecedents and consequences. For example, the therapist might ask the same couple to record the client's moods over a 2-week period, as well as the occurrence of any events that might precede or follow changes in the client's mood. *Experimental functional analysis* refers to experimentally manipulating the client's environment to test out a specific hypothesis regarding the client's behavior. For example, if a therapist suspects that a client's depression is related to her day-to-day activity level, the therapist might ask the client to vary her activity level on alternating days to assess the effect on her mood.

Each of these approaches has advantages relative to the others. Indirect functional analysis is the least costly, in terms of time and effort. In addition, it has the advantage of providing an opportunity to sample a wide range of situations and periods, so clients can provide information about the typical ways in which target behaviors relate to antecedents and consequences. However, the information obtained from indirect functional analysis is subject to biases in attention and retrospective recall, although using multiple informants can reduce the effects of this bias.

Descriptive functional analysis has the advantage that information is obtained at the time that behaviors occur, so the possibility of retrospective recall bias is reduced. However, this method is still subject to attentional and interpretive biases (i.e., clients may choose to monitor some behaviors and not others). In addition, it provides information only on the correlations among the variables of interest and does not speak to possible causal relationships. Finally, descriptive functional analysis provides information on a relatively small sample of behavior (i.e., the period during which behavior is being monitored). If the target behavior is infrequent, it may be difficult to learn about the typical ways in which the target behavior relates to its antecedents and consequences.

Experimental functional analysis is the most effective way to test hypotheses about the environmental causes of a target behavior. However, it is the most costly and time consuming of the three methods. In addition, it provides information on only a small sample of behavior, relative to the other methods, which raises the question of how generalizable findings are to other situations that arise in the client's life. Finally, it remains unknown whether experimental functional analysis adds any value beyond the information that can be obtained through the other less costly methods. Given the advantages and disadvantages of each method, we recommend that clinicians consider using combinations of all three methods when conducting a functional analysis.

Treatment Planning

Assessment data can be used to select treatment strategies in a behavioral framework in a number of ways (e.g., Nelson, 1988). First, a functional analysis can be used to identify the factors that maintain target behaviors and to select appropriate treatment interventions accordingly. For example, if a person's excessive alcohol use is reinforced by his environment (e.g., working in a bar, spending time with friends who drink to excess), treatment might include a plan to change patterns of reinforcement in the environment (e.g., finding a new job, meeting new friends) as one component of treatment.

When planning treatment on the basis of a functional analysis, it can be helpful to consider the type of problem to be changed. Kanfer and Grimm (1977) described five categories of behavior that can be targeted in behavior therapy: (a) *behavioral deficits* (e.g., poor social skills, inadequate knowledge to guide behavior, deficits in self-reinforcement, deficits in the ability to monitor or control one's behavior), (b) *behavioral excesses* (e.g., compulsive hand washing, tendencies to overmonitor one's own behavior), (c) *problems in environmental stimulus control* (e.g., sexual arousal to the sight of violence, restricted opportunities for dating because of living with parents), (d) *inappropriate self-generated stimulus control* (e.g., inaccurately labeling oneself as incapable, faulty labeling of a racing heart as dangerous), and (e) *inappropriate contingency arrangements* (e.g., desired behaviors not followed by positive consequences, undesired behaviors are reinforced, reinforcement is not contingent on behavior). Depending on the type of problem, interventions will differ. For example, for behavioral deficits, treatment is likely to focus on increasing the frequency of the target behavior, whereas for behavioral excesses, treatment is likely to focus on decreasing the behavior in question.

Another strategy for linking assessment and treatment is the *diagnostic strategy,* which involves selecting a treatment based on a *DSM–IV–TR* diagnosis (Nelson, 1988). For many *DSM–IV–TR* disorders, well-established protocols have been found to be effective for a large percentage of clients. Increasingly, behavior therapists are relying on these manualized approaches to treating psychological problems. According to Haynes (1986), the diagnostic approach is most likely to be useful when individuals with a particular disorder are relatively homogeneous, when a well-established effective treatment is available for a particular disorder, and when the costs of an idiographic assessment outweigh any additional benefits. If therapists do select treatments on the basis of a client's diagnosis, it is still often useful to conduct a functional analysis and to administer treatment protocols in a flexible way that takes into account the client's specific patterns of behavior.

Behavioral Assessment Techniques

In this section, we review commonly used behavioral assessment techniques, including clinical interviews, behavioral observation, self-monitoring, self-report scales, and psychophysiological assessment.

Clinical Interviews

Clinical interviews are a standard component of almost any psychological assessment, including a comprehensive behavioral assessment. The behavioral interview is designed to provide information needed to generate a behavioral case conceptualization, including possible target behaviors, behavioral antecedents, and consequences.

Information from the interview is used to understand both the form and the function of relevant behaviors. For example, with a client suffering from a fear of driving, a therapist might ask questions about fear triggers (e.g., situations in which the fear occurs, variables that affect the intensity of the driving fear), relevant behaviors (e.g., patterns of avoidance, use of safety behaviors), and contextual variables (e.g., accommodation by family members, deficits in driving skills). The clinician would also likely ask about other variables of interest, including the severity of the problem, its development and course, whether criteria are met for a *DSM–IV–TR* diagnosis, treatment history, medical history, client strengths, and other relevant factors. Unstructured interviews are typically used for the purpose of behavioral assessment. Witt and Elliott (1983) suggested an organizational structure for an initial unstructured behavioral interview, including these nine steps:

1. The interview agenda is discussed, and the rationale for problem identification is introduced.
2. A list of problem behaviors is collaboratively generated.
3. The frequency, intensity, and duration of each problem behavior is reviewed.
4. Antecedents and consequences of problem behaviors are identified.
5. Treatment goals are generated, and a timeline for reaching each goal is established.
6. Client strengths are identified.
7. A plan for recording behaviors is developed.
8. Methods for measuring treatment outcome are discussed.
9. The session content is reviewed, and the client agrees to the plan.

Ideally, interviews should occur with the identified client and, when appropriate, other individuals (e.g., teachers, parents, spouses, friends, colleagues) who know the client well and are familiar with the behaviors of interest. Client responses to interview questions can be used in two ways (O'Brien et al., 2005): as an indication or as a sample (e.g., tone, volume) of the client's behavior.

Despite their popularity, clinical interviews do have disadvantages: The quality of the information obtained is likely to be influenced by the clinician's interviewing skills, the client's level of awareness and understanding of factors relevant to his or her presenting problem, the client's interpretive biases and ability to recall details accurately, and many other factors.

Behavioral Observation

Direct observation of a client's behavior is the hallmark of behavioral assessment (Ollendick et al., 2004). For example, a therapist might observe a teenager interacting with his or her parents to evaluate family patterns of communication. Similarly, for someone suffering from depression, a therapist might ask the client's spouse to observe the client in social settings to evaluate the extent to which the client behaves in a withdrawn manner.

A common example of behavioral observation occurs in the context of the behavioral approach test, which is often included in the assessment of individuals with anxiety disorders. In a typical behavioral approach test, clients are asked to approach a feared object or situation, and their behavior in the situation is observed and monitored. For example, a client who is fearful of spiders might be asked to approach a spider as closely as possible while the therapist observes the client's behavior. Throughout the procedure, the client would typically provide fear ratings using a subjective units of discomfort scale ranging from 0 (*no fear or discomfort*) to 100 (*maximum fear or discomfort*). The behavioral approach test can also be used to test hypotheses about the environmental contingencies that maintain the target behavior. For example, the clinician might conduct behavioral experiments by manipulating relevant variables.

Behavioral observation has the advantage of occurring in real time, as behavior is occurring. When planning to collect data through behavioral observation, it is important to first decide what information is to be collected. Depending on the type of target behavior and the hypothesized contingencies, it might be important to sample the occurrence of events (e.g., the number of times a child cries), the duration of events (e.g., how long the child cries), the intensity of events (e.g., how loudly the child cries), the context of the events (e.g., the situations in which the child cries), or some combination of these factors. One potential problem with behavioral observation is the possibility of reactivity, which occurs when the process of assessment influences the behavior that is being assessed.

Ideally, the client should be observed in his or her natural environment, which is referred to as *naturalistic observation*. However, sometimes naturalistic observation is impractical, impossible, or unethical. In such cases, *analogue observation* may be a possibility. For example, with a client who is fearful of interviewing for a job, it may not be possible to observe the client in an actual job interview. Instead, the clinician may choose to set up a simulated interview and have the client role play the interaction. Although analogue observation may not provide information that generalizes perfectly to the real-life situation, the data obtained can still be helpful.

In some cases, the clinician directly observes the client's behavior. In other cases, someone else (e.g., a teacher, a spouse) might be assigned to the role of observer. The type of observer (participant vs. nonparticipant) can influence the type of information obtained during the assessment (O'Brien et al., 2005). *Participant observers* are individuals who observe the client's behavior while interacting with the client in some other capacity. *Nonparticipant observers* are individuals whose full attention is devoted to observing the client's behavior.

Many clinically relevant behaviors also occur naturally in the course of therapy, so that the therapist can unobtrusively observe these behaviors in the course of conducting an assessment. For instance, a client who describes frequent hostile responses in interpersonal relationships is likely to respond with hostility to the therapist at some point. The therapist can initially observe this behavior and the antecedents and consequences associated with it and use that information to inform the developing functional analysis. Later in therapy, this will provide an opportunity for intervention in the therapeutic relationship.

Self-Monitoring

Self-monitoring refers to the systematic observation of one's own behavior and the recording of one's observations, usually using diaries or structured forms. Self-monitoring has a number of different purposes, including (a) establishing a baseline level for a symptom or problem behavior, (b) measuring change in a particular behavior over time, (c) helping a client to become more aware of a problem behavior that might otherwise go unnoticed, (d) tracking the use and effects of a specific treatment strategy (e.g., using a relaxation diary to record the effects of each relaxation practice), and (e) using it as a tool to facilitate a particular therapy technique (e.g., using a thought record to challenge negative thinking or to cultivate a decentered relationship to thoughts, as described in Chapter 3).

Depending on the reason for self-monitoring, any of a number of variables can be recorded, including emotions, physical sensations, thoughts, overt behaviors, situations, activities, unwanted urges, or antecedents and consequences of target behaviors. Clients can track the frequency, intensity, duration, or latency of these variables using self-monitoring. For example, in cognitive–behavioral therapy (CBT) for panic disorder (Barlow & Craske, 2007), clients often complete a Panic Attack Record each time they experience a panic attack. On the form, they record the time and date of the panic attack, possible triggers, whether the attack was expected or unexpected, the intensity of fear experienced during the attack, and the specific symptoms experienced. The Panic Attack Record forms are relatively small, so they can fit in a pocket or purse.

Like behavioral observation, self-monitoring provides an opportunity to assess behavior as it occurs. However, because the client is responsible for recording his or her behavior, self-monitoring is relatively inexpensive and easy to use. Another advantage is that unobservable responses (e.g., panic attacks, depressive thoughts) can be sampled, which is the not the case for behavioral observation. In addition to using paper-based forms, clients can monitor their behaviors and responses on handheld computers, standard laptop or desktop computers, or web-based monitoring forms. Clients can also use audio recorders or journals to provide more detailed information. In addition, cameras can be used to capture certain types of information (e.g., taking photos of a client's apartment periodically throughout treatment for compulsive hoarding).

Before self-monitoring begins, it is important that the client receive adequate training in the self-monitoring procedures. The client should know how to use any relevant tools (e.g., monitoring forms) and should understand which variables to record. Depending on the purpose of the monitoring and the frequency with which the target behavior occurs, monitoring may involve recording each event as it occurs. However, for behaviors that occur many times throughout the day, event-by-event recording may not be practical. In such cases, another approach (e.g., recording the percentage of time that the behavior occurs during a specified period) may be used.

Although self-monitoring is a popular and useful behavioral assessment strategy, it has a number of limitations. First, the process can be influenced by client biases, errors in recording, a client's lack of awareness of the behaviors being monitored, and poor compliance. Also, therapists should inform clients that monitoring may temporarily increase distress because enhanced awareness of symptoms can be distressing at first. When clients fail to complete self-monitoring assignments, the therapist and client should assess the obstacles to monitoring (e.g., lack of motivation, lack of understanding, avoidance, pragmatic challenges such as difficulty remembering to monitor) and develop solutions that will continue to serve the intended function of monitoring (e.g., increase client awareness, provide opportunities to implement newly learned behaviors such as relaxation or behavioral activation [BA]). For an excellent review of practical issues in self-observation, see Foster, Laverty-Finch, Gizzo, and Osantowski (1999).

Self-Report Scales

Self-report questionnaires provide a quick and inexpensive way to assess a wide range of behaviors and symptoms. They vary in specificity. For example, the Symptom Checklist–90—Revised (Derogatis, 1977, 1994) is a broad measure of general psychopathology, with nine different symptom scales (e.g., Depression, Anxiety, Paranoid Ideation, Somatization). In contrast, the Social Thoughts and Beliefs Scale (Turner, Johnson, Beidel, Heiser, & Lydiard, 2003) has much more specific scope, measuring common cognitions among people with social anxiety disorder. Typically, self-report measures include a list of items that require the respondent to provide a rating on a Likert-type scale. Some measures may also include items requiring open-ended responses.

Thousands of self-report scales have been developed by psychologists and other behavioral researchers. Several comprehensive volumes have reviewed the most popular self-report scales for various forms of psychopathology, including several general books (e.g., Fischer & Corcoran, 2007; Rush, First, & Blacker, 2008) and books on specific types of scales, such as measures of anxiety (e.g., Antony, Orsillo, & Roemer, 2001), depression (e.g., Nezu, Ronan, Meadows, & McClure, 2000), school behavior (e.g., Kelley, Reitman, & Noell, 2002), sexuality (e.g., Davis, Yarber,

Bauserman, & Schreer, 1998), and social skills (e.g., Nangle, Hansen, Erdley, & Norton, 2010).

Self-report scales have a number of advantages. First, they provide a measure of the client's experience, which is a valuable component of behavioral assessment because for many problems (e.g., anxiety, depression), a primary goal of therapy is to change the client's experience. Second, self-report scales are easily administered, scored, and interpreted, with minimal cost and therapist time. Third, compared with many other behavioral assessment strategies, there is often much more available information on the reliability and validity of standard self-report scales. This is an important advantage, given the importance of using evidence-based assessment tools in clinical practice (e.g., Hunsley & Mash, 2010).

Although self-report scales are useful for assessing behaviors, symptoms, and treatment outcome, they often ignore environmental variables and tell one little about the antecedents and consequences of behavior. Therefore, they should not completely replace other behavioral assessment strategies. Also, self-report scales represent a nomothetic approach to assessment, and their psychometric properties are typically established in large groups of individuals. Therefore, it is unclear how useful the information provided by self-report scales is for any specific client.

Psychophysiological Assessment

Psychophysiological assessment involves measuring physical processes that are associated with behaviors or problems of interest. For example, in clients with anxiety disorders, heart rate is sometimes measured using portable heart rate monitors or electrocardiography to provide an objective measure of arousal, in addition to more traditional subjective ratings of fear and anxiety (Yartz & Hawk, 2001). In the assessment of insomnia, wrist actigraphy is sometimes used to measure body movements during the night using a device worn on the wrist (Savard, Savard, & Morin, 2010). Nocturnal polysomnography is another type of physiological assessment for sleep disorders, involving all-night monitoring using electroencephalography to measure electrical activity in the brain, electrooculography to measure eye movements, and electromyography to measure muscle activity

(Savard et al., 2010). Psychophysiological assessment may also include using a sphygmomanometer to measure blood pressure in the treatment of hypertension, using penile or vaginal plethysmography to measure sexual arousal when treating individuals with sexual dysfunction, or measuring skin conductance (i.e., electrodermal response, galvanic skin response) as a measure of physiological arousal.

Psychophysiological assessment is useful in that it provides another source of information that does not rely on the client or the clinician to interpret ambiguous behaviors. In addition, results of these measures are more difficult to fake than is information obtained through clinical interviews and self-report scales. However, there are also limitations to this form of assessment; principally, the meaning of data collected through psychophysiological measures is not always clear.

STRATEGIES AND TECHNIQUES

Behavioral strategies should be chosen on the basis of a functional analysis of the client's presenting problems. The techniques commonly used in behavior therapies are based in the theories outlined in Chapter 3 and should be flexibly applied with a particular client, keeping these basic principles in mind. The following sections describe some of the most commonly used behavioral strategies. A description of each technique is provided, as well as examples of the types of problems for which each strategy is typically used.

Psychoeducation

One feature that distinguishes behavior therapy from some other approaches is the fact that behavior therapy is transparent. In other words, clients are fully aware of the model underlying their treatment (e.g., the role of reinforcement in maintaining behavior) and of the rationale for each strategy. Behavior therapists may also share with their clients data from studies investigating the effectiveness of behavioral interventions. Clients learn to become their own therapists so they can continue to use behavioral strategies long after formal treatment has ended.

Psychoeducation is particularly important during the earlier sessions in behavior therapy, although the use of this strategy typically continues throughout treatment. Methods of psychoeducation may include in-session discussion, assigned readings, or research and reading on the Internet and other sources. Information shared through psychoeducation may include a behavioral model for understanding the problem, instruction in how to complete self-monitoring forms, corrective information to debunk myths and misinformation (e.g., the belief that flying is dangerous), a detailed description of the treatment process, the relationship between the behavioral model and the treatment strategies selected, and strategies for maintaining gains once treatment has ended. These strategies can increase clients' expectations for treatment success, enhance motivation, and reduce reactivity to symptoms by increasing understanding of the reasons for their occurrence.

Psychoeducation is a common component of behavioral treatment for almost every type of presenting problem. For example, in the treatment of panic disorder (e.g., Barlow & Craske, 2007), psychoeducation during the first session or two might include a discussion of the nature of anxiety and panic (e.g., that anxiety and fear are normal and are designed to help people survive when under threat, that panic attacks are a reaction to a specific stimulus even though the client may not be aware of the stimulus, that panic attacks are time limited), myths about panic attacks (e.g., that they can cause people to have a heart attack or "go crazy"), the cognitive–behavioral model of panic disorder (e.g., that panic attacks stem from a tendency to interpret benign physical sensations as dangerous), and a description of the treatment (including exposure to feared sensations and situations, cognitive strategies). Material discussed in session might be reinforced with readings assigned for homework (e.g., Antony & McCabe, 2004; Barlow & Craske, 2007).

Psychoeducation is usually included as one component of a comprehensive behavioral treatment. However, some studies have found that psychoeducation alone can be a useful intervention for a number of problems. For example, a meta-analysis of studies on psychoeducation for schizophrenia found that psychoeducation-based interventions that included families were effective for reducing symptoms and preventing relapse at 7- to 12-month follow-up, although psychoeducation directed solely at patients had only modest effects (Lincoln, Wilhelm, & Nestoriuc, 2007).

Several studies of bipolar disorder have also examined the effects of psycho-education. For example, Colom et al. (2009) found that psychoeducation was useful for preventing relapse in bipolar disorder; however, Zaretsky, Lancee, Miller, Harris, and Parikh (2008) found that CBT was significantly more effective than psychoeducation alone for maintaining improvement in individuals with this condition.

Exposure-Based Strategies

In the context of behavior therapy, the term *exposure* refers to the repeated and systematic confrontation of feared stimuli (Moscovitch, Antony, & Swinson, 2009). Many behavior therapists consider it to be an essential component of behavioral treatment for most anxiety disorders, as well as for certain related conditions. It has long been established in research with animals and humans that repeated exposure leads to a reduction in fear responding. Habituation is often cited in the literature as a mechanism to explain how exposure works, although the pattern of change seen in exposure is not consistent with what one might expect after habituation (Moscovitch et al., 2009). For example, in habituation (as it is typically defined) no new learning occurs, and there is a full reinstatement of the response after a short break; neither of these is true in the case of exposure (Tryon, 2005). Rather, models relying on the occurrence of new inhibitory associative learning or extinction seem to explain the effects of exposure much better than habituation models (for reviews, see Moscovitch et al., 2009; Tryon, 2005).

The contemporary behavior therapy literature typically refers to three types of exposure: in vivo exposure, imaginal exposure, and interoceptive exposure. *In vivo exposure* involves exposure to external situations and objects in real life (e.g., entering social situations to reduce anxiety around other people, practicing driving to overcome a fear of driving), while minimizing any forms of avoidance, such as distraction. It is a standard component of evidence-based treatments for specific phobias, social anxiety disorder, agoraphobia, obsessive–compulsive disorder (OCD), posttraumatic stress disorder (PTSD), and other problems in which an individual has an exaggerated fear of some external object or situation. Typically, the difficulty of exposures is increased gradually across sessions, although some forms of exposure therapy involve confronting the most frightening stimuli right from the start (a process sometimes referred to as *flooding*).

Imaginal exposure involves exposure in imagination to thoughts, memories, imagery, impulses, and other cognitive stimuli and is most often used in evidence-based treatments for OCD (e.g., exposure to obsessional thoughts of stabbing a loved one) and PTSD (e.g., exposure to a feared traumatic memory). Imaginal exposure may involve having the client describe a feared stimulus aloud or in writing or having the client listen to a verbal description of the feared stimulus, either in the form of an audio recording or described out loud by the therapist. The therapist encourages the client to imagine the stimulus vividly, with all of her or his senses, to maximize the new associative learning that takes place (i.e., the nonfearful associations to the range of conditioned stimuli present).

Interoceptive exposure involves purposely experiencing feared physical sensations until they are no longer frightening. It is used most often in the treatment of panic disorder. Examples of commonly used interoceptive exposure exercises include breathing through a straw to induce breathlessness, spinning in a chair to induce dizziness, and hyperventilation to induce breathlessness and dizziness.

Exposure may involve other stimuli as well. For example, exposure to visual stimuli in photos or on video is often used in the treatment of blood and needle phobias (Antony & Watling, 2006) and fears of certain animals, such as snakes, spiders, bugs, and rodents (Antony & McCabe, 2005). Exposure using computer-generated stimuli in virtual reality is also increasingly being used for the treatment of certain phobias and other anxiety disorders (Parsons & Rizzo, 2008).

Because behavioral models for disorders have begun to focus particularly on the role of avoidance of emotions (e.g., Barlow, Allen, & Choate, 2004; Mennin & Fresco, 2010) in maintaining difficulties, explicit exposure to emotional responses (which has always been a part of exposure-based treatment) has been proposed as an effective intervention. Therapists might ask clients to imagine emotional situations or view emotionally evocative film clips to reduce avoidance of their own emotional responses.

Guidelines for Effective Exposure

A number of factors have been found to affect outcomes after exposure-based treatments. First, exposure seems to work best when it is predictable (i.e., the client knows what is going to happen and when it is going to happen) and when it is under the client's control (i.e., the client controls the intensity and duration of the practice; see Antony & Swinson, 2000). Second, exposure works best when sessions are prolonged. Two-hour exposures have been found to be more effective than 30-minute exposures (Stern & Marks, 1973). However, contrary to previous assumptions, it may not be necessary for fear to decrease in any particular exposure session for a client to show improvement across sessions (Craske & Mystkowski, 2006). Third, exposure seems to work best when practices are not too spread out, particularly early in treatment (Foa, Jameson, Turner, & Payne, 1980). A number of other variables can influence the outcomes of exposure, including the extent to which the context of exposure is varied and the extent to which safety behaviors (e.g., distraction) are used during exposure practices (for a review, see Abramowitz, Deacon, & Whiteside, 2011; Antony & Swinson, 2000).

Exposure Hierarchies

Before starting exposure therapy, the therapist and client typically develop an exposure hierarchy, which is subsequently used to guide exposure practices. The hierarchy usually includes 10 to 15 situations. Each item is rated in terms of how much fear it would typically generate and how likely the client would be to avoid the situation, using a Likert-type scale (e.g., ranging from 0 to 100, where 0 = *no fear or avoidance* and 100 = *maximum fear and avoidance*). Ratings are used to determine the order of items, such that the most difficult items are at the top of the list and the less difficult items are at the bottom. Table 4.1 includes an example of an exposure hierarchy for an individual with a diagnosis of social anxiety disorder.

Response Prevention

Response prevention refers to the inhibition or blocking of a learned behavioral response to a stimulus, with the goal of breaking the association between the stimulus and the response (Nock, 2005). The process may be facilitated

Table 4.1

Exposure Hierarchy for Social Anxiety Disorder

Item	Description	Fear	Avoidance
1	Attend Rick's birthday party, where I will not know anyone except for Rick.	100	100
2	Arrange for a date with a woman I met online.	100	100
3	Eat dinner in a fancy restaurant with a single woman whom I do not know well.	100	100
4	Have lunch with three coworkers in a casual restaurant.	90	100
5	Have lunch with Rick in a casual restaurant.	80	80
6	Participate three times in a single weekly staff meeting at work.	75	90
7	Ask different people at the mall for directions (repeat for 45 min).	60	60
8	Talk to coworkers on Monday about what I did on the weekend.	50	50
9	Talk to women online through a web-based dating service.	50	50
10	Sit on a crowded bus for 45 min and make eye contact with other passengers.	45	50
11	Get my hair cut and chat with the stylist.	40	40
12	Go for a walk in my neighborhood, during the day, on a Saturday.	40	40
13	Order a pizza by phone.	25	25

Note. Fear and avoidance are rated on scales ranging from 0 to 100. *Fear* refers to the level of fear that a client expects to experience if he or she were to practice the item. *Avoidance* refers to the likelihood that he or she would avoid the situation.

by physically preventing the unwanted behavior (e.g., turning off the main water source so a client with OCD cannot wash his or her hands) or using reinforcement for not engaging in the unwanted behavior (e.g., complimenting a client for his or her success at refraining from nail biting).

Response prevention is most often discussed in the context of treating OCD, in which it is also referred to as *ritual prevention* (see the case illustration on exposure and response prevention for OCD, in the Case Illustrations section of this chapter). Compulsive rituals are believed to have the same functions as safety behaviors, avoidance, and escape—namely, to prevent the occurrence of harm and to reduce fear, anxiety, and distress. Compulsions are also thought to help maintain fear of relevant obsessional thoughts, situations, and objects. Therefore, along with exposure to feared stimuli, individuals with OCD are typically encouraged to prevent their compulsive rituals.

In addition to the treatment of OCD, response prevention is used to reduce the occurrence of safety behaviors in other anxiety-based disorders and to reduce problematic impulsive behaviors (e.g., hair pulling in trichotillomania).

Behavioral Activation for Depression

BA treatment for depression was developed by Neil Jacobson and colleagues (N. S. Jacobson, Martell, & Dimidjian, 2001; Martell, Addis, & Jacobson, 2001), although other BA protocols have also been developed (e.g., Lejuez, Hopko, & Hopko, 2001). An early dismantling study revealed that BA alone had comparable efficacy to cognitive therapy, which included both BA techniques and cognitive restructuring (N. S. Jacobson et al., 1996). Building on these findings, N. S. Jacobson and colleagues developed BA as a treatment in its own right, aimed at helping depressed individuals increase their contact with positive reinforcers and decrease patterns of avoidance and inactivity. In a randomized controlled trial, Dimidjian et al. (2006) found that BA was comparable with medication and cognitive therapy in the treatment of all levels of depression, with evidence for enhanced efficacy compared with cognitive therapy in the treatment of severe depression.

The conceptual model for BA is based on Ferster's (1973) radical behavioral model of depression. Factors external to the individual (i.e., environmental factors) are seen as potential causal and maintaining factors for depression, and intervention is aimed at these factors. Consistent with other behavioral models of depression, N. S. Jacobson et al. (2001) noted that the inactivity characteristic of depressed individuals leads to decreased contact with potential positive reinforcers, thus reducing opportunities for action to be reinforced. In addition, they noted that the inertia and withdrawal typical of depressed individuals serve a negatively reinforcing function, similar to avoidance behaviors characteristic of anxiety disorders. Despite the short-term relief that likely results from inactivity (by reducing experiences with nonreinforcing environments), these avoidance behaviors can lead to secondary problems (e.g., occupational or relational difficulties) and also limit opportunities for contact with positive reinforcers. Moreover, these avoidance patterns likely lead to disruptions in routines, which are thought to play an etiological and maintaining role in depression (Ehlers, Frank, & Kupfer, 1988).

BA directly targets avoidance behavior and routine disruptions. Therapy begins with a focus on establishing a therapeutic relationship and presenting the model of depression. Therapists work with clients to establish a goal of changing behavior rather than altering mood; clients' tendency to believe they cannot engage in an action until they feel better is gently challenged behaviorally by requesting that they try to engage in planned behaviors regardless of how they feel. Therapists and clients develop collaborative treatment goals, with a distinction made between short-term goals, many of which will be addressed during therapy, and long-term goals, only a few of which will be directly addressed during the course of treatment.

A focus on functional analysis is a critical element of this treatment. Therapist and client explore the nature of depressive symptoms, identify the triggers for depressive episodes, note how the client responds to depressive symptoms, and identify avoidant behaviors and routine disruptions. Clients are gradually taught to conduct their own functional analyses, with encouragement to do so particularly after therapy ends to prevent relapse. Drawing from the collaboratively derived functional analysis, the client and therapist develop targets for focused activation. Rather than encouraging general activity, as many behavioral approaches do, BA focuses on idiographic identification of activities that the client believes will be beneficial. Monitoring forms are used to track actions engaged in, triggers, and consequences, and assignments are modified on the basis of ongoing refinements to functional analyses.

Modification of avoidance behaviors is achieved by helping clients to identify the function of these behaviors (both the immediate relief and the longer term problems) and choose alternative coping responses. The acronym TRAP is used to help identify *triggers, responses,* and *avoidance patterns,* whereas the acronym TRAC (*trigger, response, alternative coping*) is used to help generate alternative coping responses to the same triggers and responses. Alternative coping responses frequently involve approach, rather than avoidance, behaviors. Therapist and client also work to regulate the client's routines and integrate activation strategies into regular routines, to be able to fully evaluate their impact. To maximize the impact of activation strategies, clients are encouraged to attend to their experience, particularly their immediate environment, as they engage in activities. Jacobson et al. (2001) noted that this is somewhat similar to mindfulness training in its emphasis on present-moment experience. This attention to experience is thought to increase the impact of present-moment contingencies (leading to more flexible and adaptive responding) and also to help circumvent ruminative thinking, which is thought to interfere with engagement in life. A case example using BA is presented later in this chapter.

Strategies Based on Operant Conditioning

As reviewed in Chapter 3, behavior theory assumes that behavior occurs as a function of environmental contingencies. Specifically, behaviors that are followed by desirable consequences (reinforcers) are expected to increase in frequency, and behaviors that are followed by undesirable consequences (punishment) are expected to decrease in frequency. This model helps clients and therapists to understand seemingly incomprehensible behavior, such as heroin addiction, which is maintained, in part, by negative reinforcement (i.e., additional heroin use reduces withdrawal symptoms).

Treatment strategies based on operant conditioning principles involve directly manipulating patterns of reinforcement and punishment in the client's environment. First, a detailed functional assessment must occur to identify target behaviors, behavioral antecedents, and consequences that follow these behaviors. To get the most out of operant conditioning techniques, it is helpful to identify stimuli that are likely to be reinforcing or punishing for a particular client, because these often vary across individuals (e.g., listening to a particular type of music might be a reinforcing stimulus for one individual, a punishing stimulus for another individual, and a neutral stimulus for a third individual).

If particular variables currently reinforce maladaptive behaviors, then attempts might be made to remove these reinforcers to extinguish the unwanted behavior. New reinforcers might be added to increase the frequency of desired behaviors, and punishment might used (often as a last resort) to reduce the frequency of unwanted behaviors. In the remainder of this section, we discuss reinforcement-based and punishment-based strategies, in turn.

Reinforcement-Based Strategies

Reinforcement-based techniques use procedures to reinforce desired behaviors, thereby increasing their frequency. For example, *differential reinforcement* involves reinforcing the absence of an unwanted behavior (e.g., tantrums) or reinforcing the occurrence of a desired alternative behavior (e.g., appropriate eye contact). These strategies have been used effectively with a wide range of problem behaviors, including aggression, addictions, inappropriate sexual behavior, inappropriate eating behaviors, and unwanted habits, to name a few (for a review, see Wallace & Najdowski, 2009). An example of an intervention that relies on differential reinforcement is *token economy,* a strategy (typically used in inpatient or residential settings) in which clients receive tokens for desired behaviors that can later be redeemed for various reinforcers (Donohue & Romero, 2005). Another example is *contingency management,* through which patterns of reinforcement in the client's environment are manipulated such that unwanted behaviors are no longer reinforced and desired behaviors are now reinforced. Contingency management is often used in the treatment of substance use disorders (Drossel, Garrison-Diehn, & Fisher, 2009).

Examples of differential reinforcement procedures include (a) providing housing contingent on obtaining negative drug tests each week; (b) rewarding a phobic child with stickers, small amounts of money, or other reinforcers each time he or she completes an exposure practice; (c) providing gift certificates for adhering to a weight loss program; and (d) allowing a child to watch television or play video games only after he or she has completed some required task, such as weekly household chores, homework, piano practice, or physical exercise. Social reinforcers are also an important component in the therapeutic relationship—therapists can intentionally increase the frequency of clinically desired behaviors through their own responses to clients' behavior while also consciously refraining from reinforcing behaviors that the client is trying to reduce (Kohlenberg & Tsai, 2007).

Punishment-Based Strategies

Punishment-based strategies involve exposing clients to an unpleasant consequence after an undesired behavior, with the goal of decreasing the frequency of the undesired behavior. The term *aversive conditioning* is often used to describe punishment-based techniques. A number of aversive stimuli can be used, including electrical shock or substances that induce a feeling of suffocation or nausea. For example, a drug called disulfiram (Antabuse) is sometimes used to treat alcohol dependence. Within minutes of drinking alcohol, a client taking disulfiram will experience a number of very unpleasant symptoms, including nausea, vomiting, headache, increased heart rate, and shortness of breath. Clients taking disulfiram learn very quickly not to drink alcohol while on the drug.

Other types of aversive conditioning therapy include *aversion relief,* in which a client learns to stop an aversive stimulus by performing a desired behavior (Emmelkamp & Kamphuis, 2005), and *covert sensitization,* in which the aversive stimulus occurs in imagination. The latter was designed to be used as a treatment for deviant sexual behavior (Plaud, 2005).

Punishment-based treatments should generally only be considered when other effective alternatives are not available (Wacker, Harding, Berg, Cooper-Brown, & Barretto, 2009). Although punishment-based procedures can be effective for reducing unwanted behaviors in the short term, relapse is common once the aversive consequences are withdrawn. To maximize the likelihood of long-term change, it is often helpful to include other strategies (e.g., strategies for reinforcing desired behaviors).

Cognitive Strategies

Cognitive strategies assume that distress and unpleasant emotional states (e.g., fear, anxiety, depression, anger) are triggered by negative thoughts, predictions, assumptions, and beliefs. For example, depression is assumed to stem from a consistently negative view of oneself, the future, and the world (Beck, Rush, Shaw, & Emery, 1979). Cognitive therapy addresses several levels of thinking. First is an emphasis on identifying and correcting cognitive errors or distortions, which refer to thinking errors that individuals often engage in when feeling intense anxiety, depression, or upset. Examples include all-or-nothing thinking (i.e., viewing situations in terms of opposite categories, such as flawless vs. defective), jumping to conclusions (i.e., focusing on one aspect of a situation when trying to understand it), and inappropriate blaming (i.e., using hindsight to decide what one should or should not have done; DeRubeis, Webb, Tang, & Beck, 2010). Cognitive therapy also attempts to address more deeply held beliefs, known as *core beliefs* or *schemas*. These assumptions can color how an individual views his or her world. Examples include deeply held beliefs that one is incompetent or that others cannot be trusted. Schemas can also take the form of if–then statements, such as "If I am not competent in every way, then I am a complete failure" (DeRubeis et al., 2010, p. 280).

Cognitive therapy is a collaborative process. The therapist and client work together to identify negative thoughts, to evaluate the evidence concerning these thoughts, and to arrive at more realistic ways of viewing oneself and the world. The goal of cognitive therapy is not simply to replace negative thinking with positive thinking, but rather to take an empirical approach to understanding things. Clients are encouraged to think critically, to treat their thoughts as hypotheses rather than as facts, and to examine the evidence that supports and contradicts their negative thinking. Clients are also encouraged to look at events and situations from multiple perspectives and to accept negative feelings rather than trying to actively fight or control them.

The Daily Record of Dysfunctional Thoughts (Beck et al., 1979) provides an opportunity for clients to record their negative automatic thoughts and to challenge their assumptions by considering the evidence. Several variations of this form exist, including Greenberger and Padesky's (1995) Thought Record and Antony and Norton's (2009) Anxiety Thought Record (see Figure 4.1 for an example). When completing thought records, clients are encouraged to ask themselves questions such as

- What is the evidence for my belief? What is the evidence against my belief?
- Are there other ways of viewing this situation? How might someone else view this situation?
- What if my belief were true? How could I cope with that?

In session, the therapist uses Socratic questioning to help clients challenge their beliefs. For example, if a client with panic disorder reports worrying that her racing heart might be a sign that she is having a heart attack, the therapist might ask the client whether she can think of other reasons why her heart might be racing (e.g., exercise, caffeine, stress, anxiety, paying attention to her heart rate). The therapist might also ask the client to remember back to other times when her heart was racing, to recall what the previous outcomes were, and to explore what her past experience might say about the meaning of her racing heart next time it happens. The goal of this discussion would be to help the client to become more accepting of her racing heart and to consider the likelihood of her anxious interpretation in the context of more likely benign interpretations.

Cognitive therapy was developed as a stand-alone treatment, and it is sometimes used on its own, particularly in the treatment of depression and certain anxiety disorders. However, in many cases, cognitive strategies are combined with more traditional behavioral strategies (e.g., exposure, relaxation training, stimulus control, BA) into a more comprehensive cognitive–behavioral treatment. Hundreds of studies have supported the use of cognitive strategies, either on their own or as a component of CBT. This literature is discussed in Chapter 5.

Anxiety Thought Record

Day and time	Situation	Anxiety-provoking thoughts and predictions	Anxiety before (0–100)	Alternative thoughts and predictions	Evidence and realistic conclusions	Anxiety after (0–100)

Figure 4.1

Anxiety Thought Record. From *The Anti-Anxiety Workbook: Proven Strategies to Overcome Worry, Panic, Phobias, and Obsessions* (p. 90), by M. M. Antony and P. J. Norton, 2009, New York, NY: Guilford Press. Copyright 2009 by Martin M. Antony & Peter J. Norton. Reprinted with permission.

Modeling

Modeling occurs when an individual learns a new behavior by observing others perform the behavior. For example, in the treatment of phobic children, participant modeling is often used (Ollendick & Grills, 2005). This modeling involves three main steps: (a) The client observes the therapist interacting nonfearfully with the phobic object, (b) the client and therapist interact with the phobic object together, and (c) the client interacts with the phobic object alone. In this example, modeling is used to facilitate exposure therapy. In addition to learning the specific skill or behavior, clients can learn from other aspects of the model's behavior, including the model's emotional response in the situation.

Modeling is rarely used on its own. Rather, it is typically incorporated into other behavioral strategies, including exposure, social skills training, relaxation training, self-monitoring, and problem solving, for example. In fact, modeling can be used in the context of training clients to use almost any skill. Typically, modeling involves a live demonstration of a behavior. However, it can also involve observing the behavior on film or video.

Relaxation-Based Strategies

Relaxation training is often used in behavior therapy, either as a stand-alone intervention or integrated into a multicomponent treatment package. The most extensively studied form of this intervention is progressive muscle relaxation training (Bernstein, Borkovec, & Hazlett-Stevens, 2000; E. Jacobson, 1938), particularly in the context of applied relaxation, in which progressive muscle relaxation training is taught and clients learn how to use the relaxation response effectively in their daily lives (Bernstein et al., 2000). These interventions have demonstrated efficacy for certain anxiety disorders (e.g., generalized anxiety disorder, panic disorder) and health-related problems (e.g., hypertension, headache, chronic pain, insomnia, irritable bowel syndrome, cancer chemotherapy side effects; for a review, see Bernstein et al., 2000). In addition, a limited number of studies have also supported the use of applied relaxation (typically combined with exposure-based strategies or other techniques) for social phobia, agoraphobia, PTSD, and certain specific phobias (for reviews, see Antony & Rowa, 2008; Magee, Erwin, & Heimberg, 2009; Taylor, 2000).

A common misapplication of relaxation-based strategies is to simply lead clients in a relaxation exercise in session and give some vague instructions to practice at home. Extensive relaxation exercises are only one aspect of applied relaxation and are unlikely to be effective when they are not conducted in the context of applied relaxation. Applied relaxation for anxiety (its most common use) involves three components, all of which are important: *early cue detection,* using monitoring and both verbal and imaginal review of anxiety-provoking episodes from the previous week; *intensive relaxation practice,* beginning with progressive muscle relaxation, to develop clients' ability to relax, and gradually shortening the process (see the next paragraph); and *applied relaxation* (as described by Bernstein et al., 2000), combining the skills learned in the first two components so that the client can apply relaxation in everyday life.

The process of relaxation is gradually shortened over the course of treatment, once a client has developed the ability to relax using a given strategy. Initially, individuals practice tensing and relaxing 16 muscle groups. After a few weeks of practice, the muscle groups are combined to seven muscle groups, then to four, and then a switch is made to relaxation by recall ("Remember what it felt like when you released those muscles") and finally to counting. In addition, *differential relaxation* (tensing only those muscles needed for an activity and only to the level that is necessary) and *conditioned relaxation* (pairing relaxation with a cue, e.g., the word *calm*) are introduced as the client becomes more skilled in relaxation. Each practice occurs in session with the therapist, and then the client practices regularly on his or her own at home between sessions. This process allows the client to fully develop his or her ability to relax, which is necessary for the final stage in which relaxation is applied in everyday life.

Biofeedback

Biofeedback training involves providing feedback on electrophysiological activity and training individuals to bring this activity under their control. This training may involve assessment of heart rate, facial muscle activity, finger temperature, heart rate variability, brain wave activity, or some combination of these (Gervitz, 2007). Biofeedback training is often used in the treatment of stress-related disorders and has demonstrated efficacy in the treatment of migraines and tension headaches (Spiegler & Guevremont, 2010).

Mindfulness and Acceptance-Based Strategies

As described in Chapter 3, several recent behavioral approaches to treating clinical problems explicitly emphasize cultivating acceptance of internal experiences, as opposed to efforts to change these experiences (see S. C. Hayes, Follette, & Linehan, 2004, for a book-length review of these approaches; and Roemer & Orsillo, 2009, for a therapist's guide to using these strategies). *Acceptance* has been defined in a range of ways (for a review, see Herbert et al., 2009). One behavioral definition is that acceptance involves "allowing, tolerating, embracing, experiencing, or making contact with a source of stimulation that previously provoked escape, avoidance, or aggression" (Cordova, 2001, p. 215). Acceptance-based strategies stem from theories and empirical findings that suggest that clinical problems are often characterized by reactivity to one's own internal experience (thoughts, feelings, images, sensations) and efforts to escape or avoid these experiences, which although sometimes effective in the short term, often backfire (e.g., S. C. Hayes et al., 1999; Roemer & Orsillo, 2009). The development of an alternative way of responding to internal experience (i.e., acceptance vs. judgment, criticism, and avoidance) may promote more adaptive functioning.

Acceptance is, in a sense, an implicit aspect of traditional exposure-based treatments, which encourage increased contact with, rather than avoidance of, internal and external stimuli (e.g., accepting rather than avoiding panic-related sensations in panic control treatment; Craske & Barlow, 2008). However, proponents of these acceptance-based behavior therapies have noted that behavior therapy's traditional explicit focus on change may inadvertently overlook the importance of clients learning to give up some of their futile efforts of control (e.g., over their internal experiences [S. C. Hayes, Strosahl, & Wilson, 1999] or their partner's behavior [Christensen, Wheeler, & Jacobson, 2008]) and learning to accept and validate their own experience (Linehan, 1993a). These clinical scientists have borrowed from Eastern and humanistic–experiential traditions in incorporating acceptance into their behavioral approaches to clinical problems. Acceptance should not be confused with resignation; these therapies all emphasize that an acceptance of things as they are does not preclude efforts to make changes in one's life— it may in fact facilitate making such changes.

Mindfulness-based strategies are commonly used in acceptance-based behavior therapies to help clients to cultivate acceptance as opposed to avoidance. *Mindfulness*, a concept drawn from Buddhist traditions and recently incorporated into psychological theory and therapy, has been defined as "an openhearted, moment-to-moment, nonjudgmental awareness" (Kabat-Zinn, 2005, p. 24). Rather than being seen as some kind of idealistic end state, mindfulness is a process that involves continually bringing one's attention to the present moment, again and again, while distractions continue to arise, taking one out of the present moment. As such, the practice of mindfulness involves continually developing the skill of noticing where attention is, responding with gentleness and compassion, and drawing attention back to the moment. Development of this skill has been proposed to facilitate regulation of emotions (A. M. Hayes & Feldman, 2004); to reduce depressive relapse by interrupting depressive ruminative spirals (Segal et al., 2002); to enhance cognitive, emotional, and behavioral flexibility (Shapiro, Carlson, Astin, & Freedman, 2006); and to facilitate adaptive responding to environmental contingencies (Roemer & Orsillo, 2009).

Treatments incorporate mindfulness in a number of different ways. Dialectical behavior therapy (Linehan, 1993a) teaches skills of mindfulness, using brief practices to illustrate the skills of observing, describing, and participating, nonjudgmentally, single-mindedly, and effectively. Mindfulness-based cognitive therapy (Segal et al., 2002) uses more extensive practices, such as the body scan, to help clients develop the skill of mindfulness. In all approaches, mindfulness is practiced in session, using formal exercises to develop the ability to attend with compassion or kindly awareness. Clients are then encouraged to do formal practices (i.e., setting aside time to devote to practicing mindfulness, such as sitting meditation, yoga, or other, briefer practices) at home as well. Often, clients are also encouraged to practice mindfulness informally, which involves bringing mindfulness to daily activities. Clients can first do this with neutral situations, such as washing dishes or walking to the bus stop, and gradually apply mindfulness in more emotionally charged situations such as an argument with a partner. In this way, similar to applied relaxation, the skill of mindfulness is practiced and strengthened in specific exercises and is then applied more generally to living life.

Acceptance and commitment therapy (S. C. Hayes et al., 1999) is an acceptance-based behavior therapy that was developed from the model of experiential avoidance described in Chapter 3. A host of experiential exercises and metaphors are used to help clients to defuse their internal experiences and see their thoughts and emotions as not defining them. Clients are also encouraged to begin to describe their experience differently, for instance, "I'm having the thought that I'm going to fail at this" rather than "I'm going to fail at this" to learn to be less fused with thoughts and reactions.

Acceptance (of internal responses or partners' responses) is cultivated in these treatment approaches with an explicit goal of promoting more flexible and optimal responding to situations. As such, these treatments include an explicit focus on behavioral change. By exploring what is personally meaningful to the client (values clarification), therapists identify valued actions that the client has been avoiding in the service of experiential avoidance, and the client begins to take action in these domains (K. G. Wilson & Murrell, 2004). Continued mindfulness practice (or other acceptance-based strategies) helps the client to approach valued contexts even though distressing feelings and thoughts may arise.

Randomized controlled trials have revealed that treatments that incorporate mindfulness and other acceptance-based strategies (along with other behavioral strategies) show promise in the treatment of depressive relapse, borderline personality disorder, substance dependence disorders, generalized anxiety disorder, psychotic disorders, and couples distress, although considerably more research is needed to determine active ingredients and mechanisms of action (for a review, see Roemer & Orsillo, 2009).

Emotion Regulation Skills Training

Many behavior therapies either implicitly or explicitly help clients to develop skills to more effectively recognize, understand, and respond to their own emotions (Mennin & Farach, 2007). Although regulation is sometimes thought of as only involving reduction in emotional responding, many theorists have highlighted the ways in which enhancing or clarifying emotional responding, and promoting flexible behavioral responding in the presence of emotions, are also important aspects of emotion regulation (e.g., Gratz & Roemer, 2004; Mennin & Farach, 2007). The self-monitoring included in all behavior therapies helps clients to become more aware of their emotional responses and the triggers and consequences of their emotions, and it may also help them to be more aware of the complexity of their emotional responses. Exposure-based strategies can also be thought of as facilitating regulation of fearful and anxious responding. Also, the acceptance- and mindfulness-based strategies described earlier enhance emotion regulation skills (A. M. Hayes & Feldman, 2004) and are often included in treatments that explicitly target emotion regulation skills (e.g., Gratz & Gunderson, 2006; Mennin & Fresco, 2010).

Several clinical researchers have developed specific strategies to enhance emotion regulation skills as part of treatments for specific clinical presentations. The skills training component of dialectical behavior therapy (Linehan, 1993b) includes a module focusing on emotion regulation skills that has been adapted for use across a number of clinical presentations, such as eating disorders, substance use, and anxiety disorders. Emotion regulation therapy for generalized anxiety disorder includes emotion regulation skills training as part of its integrative approach to promoting effective, flexible emotional responding (Mennin & Fresco, 2010). Emotion regulation skills training has been incorporated into behavioral treatments for deliberate self-harm (Gratz & Gunderson, 2006), adult survivors of child sexual assault (Cloitre, Koenen, Cohen, & Han, 2002), and mood and anxiety disorders (Allen, McHugh, & Barlow, 2008; Ehrenreich, Goldstein, Wright, & Barlow, 2009).

Interventions explicitly intended to enhance emotion regulation skills typically include an emphasis on helping clients to identify and clarify their emotional responses as they occur. Clients learn through monitoring, review, and imaginal rehearsal to differentiate among emotional responses and to distinguish between primary emotional responses that are direct responses to environmental events and provide important information and secondary emotional responses that may result from reactions to initial responses or efforts to avoid emotions. Clients are also taught to identify and apply strategies that can help them to respond adaptively in the presence of intense emotional responding. Randomized controlled trials provide preliminary support for the efficacy of the treatments for deliberate self-harm and adult survivors of sexual abuse that incorporate emotion regulation skills training (Cloitre et al., 2002; Gratz & Gunderson, 2006), and more research in this area is currently underway.

Social and Communication Skills Training

Relationships and social interactions are important elements of human functioning, and difficulties in these arenas can be both cause and consequence of a range of psychological problems. For instance, social skills deficits may initiate or exacerbate social anxiety, and social problems may be a consequence of alcohol dependence. Social skills training has been applied to such diverse presentations as anxiety, depression, schizophrenia, and marital distress (Segrin, 2009).

Social skills and communication training involves teaching individuals or groups to communicate more effectively. This process may include learning basic skills, such as making eye contact, ordering food in a restaurant, standing at an appropriate distance from others, and allowing others to speak without interrupting, or it may involve learning more complex skills, such as being more assertive, becoming a more effective lecturer, developing improved dating skills, or performing more effectively in job interviews. Typically, social skills training includes such strategies as psychoeducation, modeling (e.g., having a teacher, therapist, or other individual demonstrate the behavior), behavioral rehearsal or role plays, and feedback. Clients may also be videotaped while role playing a particular social interaction so they can later see how they did.

Social skills training is a standard psychological treatment for schizophrenia (e.g., Bellack, Mueser, Gingerich, & Agresta, 1997) and is often included in the treatment of social anxiety (Franklin, Jaycox, & Foa, 1999).

It is used in school-based programs (Elias & Clabby, 1992) and for helping children with severe behavior disorders (Durand, 1991). Dialectical behavior therapy includes a skills module in interpersonal effectiveness skills to address the common relational difficulties that occur for individuals with borderline personality disorder (Linehan, 1993b); these skills may also be useful for individuals with a range of other presenting problems. Finally, communication training is often included as a component of behavior treatment for couples (e.g., Lawrence, Eldridge, Christensen, & Jacobson, 1999).

Problem-Solving Training

Problem-solving theory and therapy suggest that psychological difficulties are often associated with deficits in effectively solving problems and that addressing these issues through specific interventions aimed at enhancing problem-solving abilities can therefore reduce psychological symptoms (for a review, see Nezu, 2004). Over the past 3 decades, theory and research have contributed to the development of problem-solving therapy, which has been found to be efficacious in the treatment of psychological disorders such as unipolar depression, social phobia, and schizophrenia and the distress associated with certain chronic medical disorders, including hypertension. This therapy has been presented on its own, as well as incorporated into treatment packages, and has been presented in individual, couple, and group formats (Nezu, 2004).

In this model, problem solving is conceptualized as involving two components: problem orientation and problem-solving style. *Problem orientation* refers to expectancies regarding both self-efficacy and outcome (drawing from Bandura's [1977a] self-efficacy theory). In other words, attention is paid to an individual's expectancies of his or her ability to effectively identify and implement potential solutions to problems, as well as his or her expectancy that problems are, in fact, solvable. In addition, three problem-solving styles are identified. *Rational problem solving* is seen as adaptive and follows the states of problem definition and formulation, generation of alternatives, decision making, and solution implementation and verification. In contrast, an *impulsive–careless* style is characterized by acting in response to problems without careful reflection, and an *avoidant* style is characterized by procrastination and relying too heavily on others to solve problems. Treatment is focused on cultivating a positive problem orientation (with positive self-efficacy and outcome expectancies), increasing rational problem solving, and reducing impulsive–careless and avoidant strategies (Nezu, 2004). The importance of attending to problem orientation in addition to problem-solving style is underscored by consistent findings that clinical problems are associated with negative problem orientation (reviewed in Nezu, 2004), and a dismantling study that found that problem-solving therapy that excluded training in problem orientation was significantly less efficacious than the full therapy in ameliorating depression (Nezu & Perri, 1989).

Stimulus Control Procedures

Stimulus control procedures refer to a wide range of intervention strategies that attempt to alter the function of a given stimulus, either to reduce or establish responses to a given stimulus or to alter the discriminative value of a stimulus so that it indicates that a given reinforcer will, or will not, follow a given action (Poling & Gaynor, 2009). As described in Chapter 3, many clinical problems can be understood as being under stimulus control in that a particular environmental or internal event either evokes an association (classical conditioning) or indicates that a reinforcer will occur after a given behavior (operant conditioning). Therapy therefore often focuses on altering the properties of a given stimulus.

A common application of stimulus control procedures, with empirical support, is in the treatment of insomnia (Morin et al., 2006). This therapeutic approach is aimed at increasing the degree to which bedroom environmental stimuli are associated with sleeping and decreasing the degree to which they are associated with not sleeping. As such, clients are instructed to leave the bedroom when they are unable to sleep for 15 minutes and encouraged to refrain from other activities in the bedroom besides sleep and sex (e.g., watching television, reading, eating). By systematically pairing the bedroom with sleep and not with being awake, individuals are able to sleep more readily in the bedroom.

Stimulus control procedures are also used to address substance dependence. As noted in Chapter 3, individuals with substance dependence associate a wide range of cues with using substances, leading them to experience urges in a range of contexts. Through cue exposure, clients are exposed to these cues without using the substance, leading new associations to be developed so that urges subside and cues are less likely to lead to lapses.

Stimulus control procedures are also applied to operant learning contexts (Poling & Gaynor, 2009). By drawing attention to a discriminant stimulus, such as social cues of smiling or nodding, therapy can help clients identify contexts in which social behaviors are most likely to be reinforced. This type of intervention helps clients learn to exhibit new behaviors in the context in which they are most adaptive (i.e., those in which these discriminant stimuli are present).

Relapse Prevention

Relapse prevention is a behavioral approach that was initially developed as an adjunctive treatment to address the frequency of relapse among individuals who had been successfully treated for substance and alcohol use disorders (Marlatt & Gordon, 1985). Previously, treatments typically did not explicitly address ways to maintain behavior change when the client is no longer regularly attending treatment. Relapse prevention is now a common element of many treatments that address problems with self-control. The model and techniques for relapse prevention have also been incorporated into behavioral and cognitive–behavioral treatments for anxiety and mood disorders. For all behavioral treatments, it can be extremely helpful to explicitly address ways to maintain and regain improvements after treatment is terminated. These strategies should be considered adjunctive, however, and are not a full-scale treatment in and of themselves.

Marlatt and Donovan (2005) provided an extensive description of relapse prevention strategies and evidence for their efficacy, and Newring, Loverich, Harris, and Wheeler (2009) provided a briefer overview. A central element of relapse prevention is a distinction drawn between a *lapse*, which is a recurrence in a problematic behavior, and a *relapse*, which is a return to baseline levels of the target behavior. Teaching clients this distinction can help to address the *abstinence violation effect,* in which a single incidence of a problem behavior (like a dieter's eating a piece of a chocolate cake) can seem like a such a severe threat to the behavior change that the person might as well give up efforts completely (and eat the entire cake). Although this model was developed for problems in behavioral control, it applies to clinical phenomena such as anxiety and depression as well. Clients may experience a single panic attack or a day of depressive feelings as evidence of failure and give up the strategies that have helped them to make important changes in their lives. Predicting this in advance and developing strategies to address lapses can help clients return to their effective strategies or develop new ones without giving up because an old behavior has reemerged temporarily.

Relapse prevention also involves predicting high-risk situations in which a lapse is likely to occur. Prevention includes identification of both internal and external cues that may trigger the problematic behavior to help the client predict when lapses may be likely and to prepare for or avoid them. This model also allows clients to use any lapses as new information to be analyzed to determine high-risk situations for the future. Therapists and clients work together to develop alternative behaviors at multiple points during the chain of behavior to avoid lapses and to recover from them. Relapse prevention also involves learning and practicing coping skills and strategies for achieving a balanced lifestyle.

ROLE OF THE THERAPIST–CLIENT RELATIONSHIP

Unlike many other psychotherapies, behavior therapy has traditionally not emphasized the importance of the therapeutic relationship. In 1970, Lang, Melamed, and Hart published a paper on an automated procedure for administering behavioral treatments for fear to 29 female undergraduates. In the abstract, they concluded that "an apparatus designed to administer systematic desensitization automatically was as effective as a live therapist in reducing phobic behavior, suggesting that desensitization is not dependent on a concurrent interpersonal interaction" (p. 220). Even in recent treatment development efforts, some researchers have developed computer-based attentional modification procedures to address the attentional biases that characterize many anxiety disorders (e.g., Amir, Beard, Burns, & Bomyea, 2009), implying that the therapeutic relationship may not be a necessary ingredient in behavioral interventions. A more common and less extreme approach is to suggest that a positive therapeutic alliance is a necessary condition for change, but to focus most on the technique aspect of behavioral interventions and pay little attention to therapist, client, and relationship factors. However, an extensive body of research (largely from nonbehavioral researchers) has suggested that relationship factors are important elements of treatment across theoretical orientations (e.g., Castonguay & Beutler, 2006; Norcross, 2002). Increased attention to the basic tenets of behavior theory, such as the powerful role of immediate social reinforcers in facilitating behavior change, coupled with findings from process research, has led to renewed focus on the therapeutic relationship in behavior therapies (e.g., Gilbert & Leahy, 2007; Kohlenberg & Tsai, 2007).

Therapist Factors

Therapist factors that have been identified as potentially related to treatment outcome across theoretical orientations include empathy, positive regard, congruence–genuineness, and self-disclosure (Castonguay & Beutler, 2006). From a behavioral perspective, these characteristics may promote change for a number of reasons, including that (a) they are used to socially reinforce desired behaviors; (b) they provide experiences that challenge interpersonal expectancies, promoting greater flexibility in interpersonal behavior outside of treatment; (c) they provide models of interpersonal behavior that promote an expanded interpersonal repertoire outside of therapy; (d) they promote engagement in therapy and collaboration on treatment goals, thus enhancing compliance with homework assignments; and (e) they facilitate emotional engagement, which promotes activation of fear structures so that new information can be incorporated.

In their review of 3 decades of research on the relationship between therapist and client interpersonal behaviors and outcome in CBT, Keijsers, Schaap, and Hoogduin (2000) concluded that there is consistent evidence for a moderate relationship between the Rogerian therapist variables (i.e., warmth, empathy, positive regard, and genuineness) and outcome in CBT. They also noted that studies have shown that cognitive–behavioral therapists display as much positive regard and empathy as, and higher levels of emotional support than, insight-oriented therapists. Keijsers et al. noted that although most studies are correlational in nature and use self-report of therapist variables, some experimental analogue studies have shown that these therapist behaviors enhance participant learning. The data suggest, therefore, that warmth, empathy, positive regard, and genuineness are important therapist behaviors in behavior therapies. However, the mechanisms underlying these associations have not yet been identified.

Keijsers et al. (2000) went on to note that some evidence suggests that client perceptions of how self-confident, skilled, and active the therapist is also predict outcome in CBT. They noted that these studies assessed client perception of these attributes rather than the attributes themselves. These findings may in fact reflect a client characteristic rather than a therapist one, in that clients who attribute these characteristics to therapists may be more likely to have positive expectancies and to engage in treatment more actively.

Client Factors

Client factors that have been hypothesized to play an important role in CBT outcome include motivation (Miller, 1985), expectancies for change, homework compliance, interpersonal problems (e.g., Borkovec, Newman, Pincus, & Lytle, 2002), and openness to discussing problems. Client openness may facilitate therapy by contributing to depth of emotional experiencing. Although depth of emotional experiencing has been studied more fully in the context of other theoretical orientations, as noted earlier, emotional activation is thought to facilitate the activation of associative networks, allowing new learning to occur (Foa & Kozak, 1986).

Keijsers et al. (2000) concluded that no client factors have been consistently established as related to outcome in CBT. However, they reported some indication that clients' openness to discussing their problems may be related to outcome. In addition, clients' perceptions of their own motivation may predict outcome, although therapist or observer assessments of motivation are not reliably associated with outcome. However, although many studies have investigated the role of homework compliance in outcome, the data do not suggest that this factor is consistently related to outcome. Keijsers et al. noted that this may be due to failures in assessing compliance meaningfully (e.g., assessing quality of compliance). Expectancy has also not been consistently related to outcome (e.g., Borkovec et al., 2002). In one study that investigated whether pretreatment for interpersonal problems predicted outcome in a cognitive–behavioral treatment for generalized anxiety disorder, only a small proportion of the identified interpersonal dimensions were significantly related to outcome, although remaining interpersonal problems at posttreatment were more reliably associated with poorer outcomes, suggesting that failure to address these problems may affect outcome (Borkovec et al., 2002).

Relationship Factors

One of the most researched aspects of the therapeutic relationship is the working (or therapeutic) alliance. In the most commonly used definition, *working alliance* refers to the strength and quality of the collaborative relationship between the therapist and the client, encompassing both the affective bond between the two and their agreement on the goals of therapy and the tasks required to meet these goals (adapted from Horvath & Bedi, 2002). As Keijsers et al. (2000) reviewed, in research that uses measures that assess this operational definition, the working alliance has consistently been moderately associated with outcome in CBT, with associations stronger when the alliance is reported by clients than by therapists. They also reported that CBT has thus far been associated with comparable or higher working alliance ratings to insight-oriented or psychodynamic therapies.

There are many reasons that working alliance may predict outcome in behavior therapies. A strong alliance may facilitate engagement in exposure exercises necessary for new learning (S. A. Hayes, Hope, VanDyke, & Heimberg, 2007), as well as engagement in other homework assignments.

It may also provide an optimal context for new interpersonal learning (Kohlenberg & Tsai, 2007), as well as emotional openness that facilitates learning of new emotional associations. Further research is needed to determine the precise mechanisms through which a strong alliance facilitates change in behavior therapies, as well as how therapist and client factors may affect the development of a strong alliance. In addition, research is needed on the process of repairing ruptures in alliance (Safran, Muran, Samstag, & Stevens, 2002) in the context of behavior therapy. The behavioral focus on clearly developing a consensual model for treatment, repeatedly revisiting goals and tasks of therapy, and addressing any disagreements in shared understandings may help to address ruptures as they occur, although this has not yet been demonstrated empirically.

CASE ILLUSTRATIONS

Following are three cases illustrating the use of behavioral treatments. The first demonstrates the use of exposure and response prevention in the treatment of OCD. The second illustrates the use of BA for the treatment of depression. The third provides an example of how acceptance-based behavior therapy might be used to treat alcohol dependence.

Exposure and Response Prevention for OCD

Exposure and response prevention (also known as *exposure and ritual prevention*, or ERP) is the best-studied psychological treatment for OCD and is recommended as a first-line treatment for OCD in practice guidelines published by both the American Psychiatric Association (2007) and the Canadian Psychological Association (Swinson et al., 2006). In fact, behavioral treatments (including ERP and cognitive–behavioral strategies) are the only psychological treatments that are empirically supported for the treatment of OCD. ERP involves graduated exposure to feared situations, thoughts, and images, combined with prevention of compulsive rituals and related safety behaviors. A detailed description of ERP, as well as a review of empirical studies, is available elsewhere (Rowa, Antony, & Swinson, 2007).

Parker was a 16-year-old, White high school student who presented for treatment of aggressive and religious obsessions, as well as compulsions involving checking and repeating. He grew up in a traditional Catholic family, although he reported that he and his family were less religious in recent years than they had been in the past. For as long as he could remember, he experienced occasional superstitious thoughts and behaviors. For example, from time to time he would have intrusive thoughts about harm coming to a close friend or family member and would "touch wood" to keep his loved ones safe. Since age 12, the frequency of his intrusive thoughts and superstitious rituals had gradually increased, so that by the time he presented for treatment they were occurring throughout the day and having a significant impact on his schoolwork and relationships.

A detailed functional assessment revealed two main categories of fear triggers and compulsions. The first set of symptoms involved a fear of stimuli related to Satan, hell, and other symbols of evil and the occult. For example, Parker became very frightened when encountering words and phrases such as *devil, ghost, Satan, hell, sin, Black Sabbath,* and *666,* either in writing, verbally, or mentally (in the form of thoughts and mental imagery). Other triggers included visual images that reminded him of these cues, such as horror movies, pictures of Satan, and people who dressed in a Goth style. He avoided these stimuli whenever possible, as well as situations in which he might encounter these stimuli (e.g., reading novels, watching television, seeing movies, walking in parts of town). In response to encountering these triggers, either in reality or mentally, Parker touched his cross several times, replaced the feared words in his mind (e.g., *Satan, hell*) with safe words (e.g., *God, Jesus, heaven*), and repeated a series of prayers until his fear was reduced. If a feared thought entered his mind while he was engaging in some behavior (e.g., turning on a light, opening a door), he felt compelled to repeat the behavior until he could do it without having the feared thought.

In addition to his religious obsessions and compulsions, Parker also reported intrusive thoughts about harming loved ones, including his parents, siblings, friends, and dog, with knives, scissors, pens, and other sharp objects. He generally avoided being around sharp items whenever he could. He also felt compelled to warn other people whenever he had an intrusive thought about harming them. His aggressive thoughts occurred daily, and in response to these thoughts he used a number of strategies to reduce his anxiety, including suppressing his thoughts, confessing his thoughts to others, seeking reassurance from loved ones, distracting himself, and avoiding any situations that might trigger the thoughts (e.g., being around other people while holding a sharp object). His parents and girlfriend habitually provided reassurance to Parker to that he was not going to act on his thoughts.

Parker's first three treatment sessions were conducted weekly. At Session 1, a detailed list of situational and mental triggers, intrusive thoughts and images, and compulsive rituals (including both overt rituals and mental rituals) was generated. The Yale–Brown Obsessive Compulsive Scale (Goodman, Price, Rasmussen, Mazure, Delgado, et al., 1989; Goodman, Price, Rasmussen, Mazure, Fleischmann, et al., 1989) was administered to establish a baseline assessment of his OCD severity. His score was 30, which is in the severe range. Parker also began to complete monitoring forms on which he recorded the frequency and severity of his intrusive thoughts, the intensity of his urges to engage in compulsions, and any times when he actually engaged in a compulsive ritual. He continued to complete these forms for the remainder of his treatment. Parker was also asked to begin reading *Getting Over OCD* (Abramowitz, 2009), one of several excellent self-help workbooks describing evidence-based treatments for OCD.

At Session 2, Parker was introduced to the principles of ERP. A behavioral model of OCD was presented, with an emphasis on the functional relationship between his fear triggers (including situations and intrusive thoughts and images) and the behaviors he used to reduce his fear (including compulsions, avoidance, and attempts to suppress frightening thoughts). Although his compulsions and other safety behaviors were effective in reducing his fear in the short term, they were assumed to help maintain his OCD over the long term by preventing the extinction of fear. Parker was taught that to overcome his OCD it would be necessary to start confronting the situations he fears, experiencing his intrusive thoughts without trying to suppress them, and refraining from using compulsions to manage his anxiety.

For the purpose of planning exposure exercises, Parker's religious concerns and his intrusive thoughts about harming others were considered separately. Two distinct exposure hierarchies (each with 15 items) were developed—one for his religious obsessions and one for his concerns involving harming others. The hierarchies were developed during Session 2 and at the beginning of Session 3. Examples of items from his hierarchies are presented in Exhibit 4.1.

Parker and his therapist agreed to start working on his obsessions about harming others first. The frequency of sessions was increased to twice per week to provide adequate support to Parker during the initial stages of treatment. During Session 3, he began practicing items near the middle of his hierarchy (e.g., cutting up newspapers with scissors in front of his therapist), although at home he initially practiced easier items from

---

Exhibit 4.1

Examples of Items From Parker's Exposure Hierarchies

Exposure Hierarchy for Religious Obsessions

- Write out the phrase "I am Satan" repeatedly for 30 min (Item 1).
- Watch scary scenes from "The Exorcist" on YouTube repeatedly for 60 min (Item 4).
- Use the words *hell* and *ghost* repeatedly while talking to my girlfriend for 30 min (Item 7).
- Look at photos of Goths on the Web for 30 min (Item 8).
- Listen to my girlfriend say the words *hell* and *ghost* repeatedly while talking to me for 30 min (Item 12).

Exposure Hierarchy for Obsessions About Harming Others

- Hold a kitchen knife to my mother's back for 30 min (Item 1).
- Cut up vegetables with my father sitting with his back to me in the kitchen for 45 min (Item 4).
- Cut up a newspaper with scissors with my girlfriend sitting facing me for 45 min (Item 6).
- Imagine stabbing my brother with a pen for 30 min (Item 9).
- Play with my dog while holding a pen for 30 min (Item 11).

---

the bottom third of his list. Parker was asked to practice exposures at home for at least an hour per day, at least 5 days per week, and to refrain from all compulsive rituals and attempts to suppress thoughts related to harming others. He was instructed to practice exposure items repeatedly until they became easier and then to move to the next item on his hierarchy. Parker and his therapist agreed to have brief phone calls daily during the first week after exposures began. At the fifth session, Parker's parents and girlfriend joined him. Although he had asked them to stop providing reassurance (as suggested by his therapist), they were continuing to reassure him that they knew he was not going to harm them. Parker and his therapist agreed that bringing them in for one session to encourage them to stop all reassurance would be helpful.

By Session 8, Parker was able to practice the most difficult items on his "harming others" hierarchy in the therapist's office, and he was beginning to see a reduction in fear for all items practiced both at home and in his sessions. He and his therapist agreed to introduce exposures related to his religious obsessions at that point. For example, Parker was asked to post signs on his bedroom wall containing feared words (e.g., *Satan, hell*) and phrases (e.g., *I love Satan*) and to refrain from using any rituals (e.g., prayer, touching his cross) to reduce his fear.

Initially, Parker was reluctant to follow through with these practices, wondering whether they might be misinterpreted by God as a sign that he really did love Satan. His parents also had concerns about posting the signs in his room. The family decided to consult with their priest, who encouraged them to follow through with the treatment. He explained to Parker and his parents that God would understand that the exposures were designed to treat Parker's OCD and were not a sign of Satan worship. In the first week of exposure to religious cues, Parker and his therapist reintroduced daily phone calls to ensure that Parker was following through with practices and refraining from engaging in compulsions whenever possible.

After 12 sessions, Parker's OCD symptoms had reduced considerably. His score on the Yale–Brown Obsessive Compulsive Scale (Goodman, Price, Rasmussen, Mazure, Delgado, et al., 1989; Goodman, Price, Rasmussen, Mazure, Fleischmann, et al., 1989) had decreased to 14 (in the mild to moderate range). Sessions were reduced in frequency to once per week for the next four meetings and then to once every 2 weeks for another two sessions. Treatment was terminated when Parker's Yale–Brown Obsessive Compulsive Scale score was 8. He still had occasional intrusive thoughts, in relation both to hurting others and to his religious obsessions, but they now were only mildly distressing and no longer caused significant impairment. By the end of treatment, Parker rarely engaged in compulsive rituals. However, he remained worried that his problems could return in the future. He and his therapist agreed to meet again in 3 months to check on his progress. At that time, he was much more confident in his ability to maintain his gains going forward.

Behavioral Activation for Major Depressive Disorder

Santiago-Rivera et al. (2008) suggested that BA (Martell et al., 2001) may be an effective intervention for depression among Latinos and Latinas because of its emphasis on environmental factors and behavior change. They reviewed literature that details the number of environmental causes that may be associated with depression among Latinos and Latinas and also noted that depressive symptoms in this population may be associated with realistic appraisal of lack of control rather than cognitive distortions that could be the target of intervention. This case illustration draws from their suggestions for cultural adaptation of BA in the treatment of depression in a Latino client.

Pedro was a 38-year-old bilingual Latino man who presented for treatment reporting depressive symptoms, hopelessness, loss of interest in things he used to enjoy, and increased appetite and weight gain. He was married, with 10- and 12-year-old daughters and a 14-year-old son. He and his wife had immigrated to the United States from Mexico 15 years prior; his sister and brother-in-law lived nearby, and the rest of his family still lived in Mexico. He was going to school to complete his bachelor's degree while also working a part-time job to help support his family. He reported difficulties keeping up with his school work and growing distance in his marriage. His wife was also working part time to help support the family. He also reported feeling distant from his children. In the initial session, Pedro expressed a lot of disappointment in himself for his current level of functioning and a great deal of self-criticism and rumination about the ways he was not living up to his own expectations. He expressed feelings of guilt for not enjoying the opportunities available to him when other family members did not have the same benefits he had.

Treatment with Pedro began with a clinical assessment that included self-report measures, initial monitoring of depressive symptoms, and an extensive intake that assessed symptoms and contextual factors that might be associated with presenting problems. Pedro's expectations about therapy, including his hopes and fears, were also assessed. His therapist also asked about Pedro's experiences of acculturative stress (e.g., what the process of moving to the United States was like for him, any challenges he faced in adjusting), as well as experiences of racism and discrimination he had experienced during his time in the United States, using open-ended questions that sensitively addressed these topics and conveyed her understanding that these kinds of experiences are common among immigrants and members of ethnic minority groups. Efforts were made to focus on specific goals that Pedro had for therapy, with attention to cultural values. The therapist used her general knowledge of values that might play a role in Pedro's experience given his identity as a Mexican American immigrant (e.g., acculturative stress, experiences of discrimination, values of family connectedness [*familismo*], and the male role of providing for the family and being responsible [*machismo*]) but was careful to ask about the specific role of these values in Pedro's life, rather than assuming the importance of each issue because of his ethnic background. To get a sense of the routines in his life and his level of activity or lack thereof, the therapist asked Pedro to describe a typical day. She also acknowledged cultural differences between herself and Pedro and invited him to let her know if she seemed to be misunderstanding his experience in any way.

Pedro's symptoms met criteria for major depressive disorder. Through the clinical interview, he recognized that although he had experienced some dysphoric feelings since moving to the United States, his symptoms had become more severe during the past year when he had begun pursuing a degree and left his job. Exploration of other environmental changes that had accompanied this change in jobs revealed that Pedro had worked with several Mexican Americans, whom he had known for many years, whereas he was now taking classes with people he did not know and with whom he did not interact. He reported experiences of discrimination in the context of school. In addition, his daily routine had changed when he started school; he had gone from a very regular routine to a more erratic one. Some nights he stayed up late doing work for his classes and then slept late in the morning, and other nights he went to bed earlier so that he could wake up in time for a morning class. On weekends, he regularly stayed up late studying and slept late in the mornings. Staying up late and subsequently sleeping late, particularly on the weekends, also reduced his time with his family because he missed family activities, such as attending church on Sundays.

Review of monitoring forms helped to identify the patterns of responding that were contributing to Pedro's depression and isolation. For instance, demands from school were a significant trigger. When he perceived these demands (trigger), he responded with hopelessness, depressed feelings, and self-criticism (response). This typically led to his procrastinating by surfing the Internet or watching television (avoidance pattern). This avoidance further fueled his self-criticism and sense of hopelessness and also resulted in his staying up late to get his work done, which disrupted his sleep routine and reduced his time with his family. Pedro also described cognitive triggers, such as thoughts that he was not supporting his family well, which led to feelings of sadness and shame, which in turn led him to avoid interpersonal interactions with his family and friends.

A central focus in the beginning of therapy was developing a shared understanding of Pedro's depressive symptoms that emphasized the role of environmental factors and learned avoidance patterns in his continued distress. The therapist pointed out the numerous stressors that Pedro was facing in his pursuit of his degree (including experiences of discrimination) and highlighted the learned avoidance patterns that had naturally evolved in response to these triggers, but were perpetuating the cycle of depression. This model was a novel way of understanding depression for Pedro; however, he could see the way it described the pattern of his experience. He reported experiencing relief as he began to see his depressive symptoms as resulting from environmental factors rather than from his own limitations. Although he was concerned he would not be able to change his behavior patterns, he responded to the idea of taking action from the "outside in" rather than waiting to feel like engaging in a particular action. Pedro's wife was also invited to a session, and Pedro shared this conceptualization with her and described the treatment approach so that she was able to better understand his experience and support his efforts at behavior change.

Over the course of treatment, Pedro and the therapist worked together to identify activities for focused activation, including making plans to see his brother-in-law and friends from his old job, whom he had been avoiding; waking up to go to church with his family; planning activities with his wife and children, regardless of how he was feeling; initiating social contact with people in his class; and engaging in regular exercise. By monitoring his activities and responses, Pedro was able to determine which activities were associated with improvements in his mood, or improved functioning despite his mood, and made these activities part of his regular routine. Attention was also paid to routine regulation; the therapist suggested that Pedro try to go to sleep at a set time each night and wake up at a set time to reduce the dysregulation that was likely resulting from his erratic sleep pattern. Pedro was initially reluctant to alter his patterns for fear that it would negatively affect his ability to do his school work. The therapist validated his concern and asked him whether he would be willing to try out a more regular routine for a few weeks to see whether it had the feared effects, while also addressing his avoidance pattern regarding his school work to minimize any risk to his academic performance (described in the next paragraph). Because Pedro could see the way in which his sleep pattern might be making his mood more problematic, he agreed to give this a try temporarily.

Pedro learned to notice when he was having responses to triggers of school stress and made the choice to approach his school work instead of avoiding it. He found that approaching his work, even when he really did not feel like it, actually improved his mood. Over time, he was able to complete his school work during a set period and leave time at the end of the night to spend with his wife, which began to reduce the distance and conflict in their relationship. Gradually, Pedro noted significant improvements in his mood, a renewed interest in activities, and a renewed sense of connection with his family members.

Acceptance-Based Behavioral Therapy for Alcohol Dependence

Randomized controlled trials have suggested that acceptance and commitment therapy holds promise in the treatment of substance dependence disorders (e.g., Hayes, Wilson, et al., 2004). This case illustration draws from acceptance and commitment therapy and other acceptance-based behavioral therapies in treating a woman with alcohol dependence.

Audrey was a 48-year-old, White, divorced woman who presented for therapy with an extensive history of alcohol dependence. She reported that she had started drinking as an adolescent and drank regularly early in her marriage, along with her husband. Five years into her marriage, her husband stopped drinking excessively and encouraged her to do the same. Initially, Audrey was able to significantly cut down on her alcohol consumption. However, 5 years later, as she began dealing with the stress of her mother's chronic illness and increased stress at work, she began drinking regularly again. Her drinking was associated with increased conflict in her marriage and reduced contact with her family members. Eventually, her husband decided that he could not live with her because of her drinking, and they divorced. Audrey continued drinking, both alone and with friends; however, it began to significantly affect her ability to do her job, and she had begun to fear losing her job, which prompted her to come to therapy.

In addition to an initial clinical interview, the therapist asked Audrey to monitor her drinking and to notice the cues that preceded her drinking behavior. As they reviewed these forms together, a clear pattern emerged. Although drinking had become a habit for Audrey, so that she often reached for a drink without thinking about it, her drinking most often started in response to feelings of anxiety or sadness or thoughts such as "I am such a failure." These feelings dissipated as she drank, yet they often returned the next day, exacerbated by the self-criticism and judgment that followed her excessive drinking. This pattern was directly contributing to her problems at work. She had gotten behind on projects, in part because she regularly came to work late as a result of being hung over in the morning. When she had thoughts about how she needed to go to bed early on a given night, she immediately experienced feelings of shame about her work performance and had thoughts that she was a failure and hopeless. She drank in response to these triggers, causing her to stay up late again and wake up hung over. Thus, she had been unable to change her drinking behavior, despite genuinely wanting to improve her performance at work.

The therapist described the ubiquity of experiential avoidance and the social messages that often make people feel like they should be able to control their internal experiences, so that many people learn to engage in these kinds of efforts to experientially avoid, routinely worsening rather than alleviating their suffering. Audrey responded to the model positively but expressed fear that she would not be able to handle experiencing her emotions. She also worried that she would not be able to change her behaviors, given her past failures in attempting to make change.

Drawing from acceptance and commitment and mindfulness-based therapies, the therapist worked with Audrey to help her reduce her fusion (or entanglement) with her internal experiences. She had Audrey engage in mindfulness exercises in session and between sessions, beginning with mindfulness of sensations and then practicing mindfulness of thoughts and feelings to cultivate an ability to defuse or decenter from these experiences. The therapist also introduced defusion exercises, such as saying "I'm having the thought that . . . " as a way of noticing that thoughts are thoughts, rather than the statements of fact they present themselves as. The concept of "urge surfing" was also introduced so that Audrey could notice her urges to drink without fighting against them or drinking as a result of having the urge (Marlatt & Donovan, 2005). Metaphors were used to illustrate the ways in which a struggle with internal experiences can be altered to a stance of willingness. For instance, Audrey was asked to imagine throwing a party and wanting everyone to be welcome, but then discovering that an annoying neighbor planned to attend ("Joe the Bum" metaphor from acceptance and commitment therapy; S. C. Hayes et al., 1999). Together the therapist and Audrey explored various ways of trying to keep this annoying neighbor from ruining the party but realized that any efforts to limit the neighbor would result in limiting Audrey's experience of the party. Willingness to have the neighbor at the party would give Audrey the freedom to engage in being at the party. Audrey was able to see how a similar response to her own internal experiences would allow her to engage more fully in her life.

The therapist also spent time in initial sessions exploring Audrey's values, or what was important to her (K. G. Wilson & Murrell, 2004). In the initial assessment, Audrey was clearly disconnected from what was important to her. She was able to identify goals, such as not losing her job, but she had trouble describing why her job was important to her, other than so that she could pay her rent. She also identified wanting to be able to handle stress. The therapist asked Audrey to engage in a series of writing assignments, first exploring how drinking had gotten in the way of her living the life she wanted to live and then exploring how she would want to live her life if there were no obstacles at all. These topics were also explored in therapy through various exercises, such as asking Audrey to imagine what she would want her gravestone to say (as a way of assessing what she wanted her life to stand for) or asking her to imagine what she would do in her life if she were able to handle stress.

The process of values clarification was very emotional for Audrey because she began to realize the ways in which she was not living the life she wanted to be living. She was able to use the mindfulness skills she had been developing to stay with her experience as she and her therapist began to identify the ways she wanted to be in the world. For instance, she described wanting to be available to her friends and provide care and understanding, something she was not always able to do because of her drinking behavior. She also realized that she missed the emotional intimacy she had experienced in the context of her marriage and that she wanted to find that type of connection again, something she had been unaware of before beginning therapy. She also identified that she valued being a part of a team at work and that she wanted to do her part in team projects, to contribute to the team and support her coworkers. Through this process, Audrey identified how strongly she valued social connectedness and realized that her drinking friends had become her only source of social connection, which was another reason it had become so difficult to stop drinking. Drinking had also become the only context in which she felt able to open up to people, although she wanted to be able to be emotionally vulnerable without drinking.

Once her valued directions had been identified, Audrey and her therapist chose valued actions for her to engage in each week. Audrey chose the behavior of going to sleep earlier as an action connected to her value of being a responsible member of her team at work. She was able to use her mindfulness skills to notice the thoughts that arose about her own failures and her feeling of shame and to refrain from drinking in response to them, so that she could go to sleep and wake up early and feel good enough to get to work and work on her projects. She also began making plans with acquaintances who did not drink socially, so that she could meet her value of social connectedness without perpetuating her drinking behavior. She brought mindfulness to these interactions so that she could be more fully engaged in these valued connections. Over time, she experienced reinforcement from these valued actions as her work improved and she made new friends who did not encourage her excessive drinking behavior. As these changes became more stable and she found herself increasingly willing to have whatever internal experiences arose in her pursuit of valued actions, she began online dating. Although this new situation was associated with anxious thoughts and feelings, Audrey was able to mindfully notice them without becoming fused with them and still engage in actions that were meaningful to her. She noticed that she had strong urges to drink when she went on dates, but she was able to refrain from following these urges ("surf" them) because she was enjoying the enhanced experience of life she was having now that she no longer drank excessively.

When Audrey was prepared to end therapy, her therapist spent time on relapse prevention to prepare her for future experiences that might lead to increases in her urges and distress and decreases in her ability to defuse from these experiences and choose valued actions instead of reactions to reduce her distress. The therapist emphasized the importance of continued attention to maintaining her new relationship with her internal experiences and of continuing to examine her values and choose valued actions.

OBSTACLES AND CHALLENGES
IN BEHAVIOR THERAPY

Perhaps the biggest challenge in behavior therapy has been the difficulty in disseminating behavioral treatments to practicing clinicians and ensuring that these interventions are available for those who need them. We begin this section with a discussion of barriers to dissemination of behavior therapies, and of evidence-based psychological treatments more broadly. Next, we discuss challenges to client motivation, compliance, and ambivalence about treatment.

Dissemination and Access to Therapists
With Specialized Training

Dozens of empirically supported treatments have emerged over the past few decades, and most of them fall under the broad umbrella of behavioral and cognitive–behavioral therapies (Chambless et al., 1996, 1998; Task Force on Promotion and Dissemination of Psychological Procedures, 1995). Unfortunately, however, interventions with the most empirical support are often not the treatments that clients receive in routine clinical practice. For example, Becker, Zayfert, and Anderson (2004) surveyed 852 randomly selected psychologists from three states regarding their use of exposure-based treatments for PTSD, an approach that is supported by numerous randomized controlled trials. In this sample, only 28.5% of participants had some previous training in imaginal exposure for PTSD, 27.1% had training in in vivo exposure for PTSD, and 12.5% had training in exposure for other anxiety disorders. Of those trained to use imaginal exposure for PTSD, 54% used it occasionally, and only 29% used it with more than half of their clients with PTSD. The most common reason given for limiting their use of imaginal exposure when treating PTSD was a lack of adequate training, even among those who identified "behavioral/CBT" as their primary orientation. These findings suggest that psychotherapists may not be adequately trained in evidence-based behavioral treatments.

There is further evidence that empirical research findings have had only a limited impact on the community practice of psychotherapy. In a survey of more than 2,600 psychotherapists in the United States and Canada, J. M. Cook, Schnurr, Biyanova, and Coyne (2009) found that data from well-designed randomized clinical trials have a relatively small effect on how psychological disorders are treated by mental health providers. Instead, the most frequently reported influences on clinical practice were past mentors, books, training in graduate school, and informal discussions with colleagues. Given how few psychotherapists use evidence-based approaches, Chorpita and Regan (2009) argued that research on psychological treatments needs to go beyond its current focus on whether psychological treatments work and why they work and should now begin to emphasize the best ways to disseminate effective psychological treatments if there is going to be any significant impact on public health.

Compliance and Motivation

Perhaps the most commonly encountered challenge that arises during behavior therapy is a suboptimal level of compliance with treatment procedures, which can stem from any of a number of sources. For example, clients may fail to comply with treatment because they do not understand the rationale or procedures (e.g., confusion over how to complete monitoring). Similarly, a busy schedule may prevent some clients from completing their homework. Fear of possible harm from the treatment procedures (e.g., having a heart attack while completing interoceptive exposure exercises) may also undermine compliance, as can certain therapist behaviors. For example, failing to adequately review homework may send a message to the client that homework is not important.

A common source of noncompliance is ambivalence about changing the identified target behavior. This is particularly likely if a behavior to be decreased is inherently reinforcing (e.g., substance use) or if the client has sought treatment only because of pressure from an external source (e.g., a spouse or a court order) rather than an intrinsic desire to change. Because behavior therapy often requires clients to increase the frequency of behaviors that are unpleasant (e.g., increasing activity levels when feeling depressed and exhausted, confronting feared stimuli in the treatment of anxiety disorders) or to decrease behaviors they enjoy (e.g., reducing gambling or overeating), some level of engagement and motivation is necessary.

The most skilled behavior therapists use a range of strategies to enhance clients' commitment to the treatment process. For example, they may arrange brief phone contacts between sessions or include family members in the treatment to ensure that clients are engaged in the treatment outside of the therapist's office. Therapists may also work with the client to problem solve around any obstacles that interfere with treatment (e.g., scheduling conflicts). In the case of exposure therapy, therapists try to ensure that exposure practices occur at an optimal pace. Taking steps too slowly may lead to slower improvements, which may in turn lead to a loss of motivation. However, taking steps too quickly may lead to overwhelming fear during exposure, which may negatively affect compliance and motivation. An important role of the therapist is to identify possible obstacles and threats to motivation and to help the client overcome these challenges.

In recent years, motivational interviewing has emerged as a helpful intervention for resolving ambivalence and increasing motivation for treatment. It has been used successfully in the treatment of substance use disorders and to improve compliance with health behaviors (e.g., exercise, medication compliance). Data are also emerging regarding the treatment of eating disorders, anxiety disorders, and other conditions. Typically, motivational interviewing is administered in one to three sessions, immediately before the onset of another evidence-based treatment (e.g., CBT), although research has supported the use of motivational interviewing as a stand-alone treatment for substance use disorders. Several books have summarized research findings on motivational interviewing and described how to administer this intervention (Arkowitz, Westra, Miller, & Rollnick, 2008; Miller & Rollnick, 2002; Rollnick, Miller, & Butler, 2008; Rosengren, 2009). Briefly, motivational interviewing focuses on helping clients to consider the costs and benefits of changing, to identify intrinsic reasons for changing, and to explore other factors that contribute to ambivalence about treatment. Unlike behavior therapy, which tends to be very directive, motivational interviewing is an evidence-based, client-centered approach that refrains from any assumptions regarding whether a client should engage in treatment at a given time.

5

Evaluation

Behavior therapy is among the best-studied psychotherapies and has been found to be useful for a wide range of problems. In this chapter, we review the empirical basis of behavior therapy, including research regarding several specific disorders, research examining the limitations of behavior therapy, and research on the use of behavior therapy with clients from diverse backgrounds.

EVIDENCE SUPPORTING BEHAVIOR THERAPY

No psychotherapy has been subjected to as much research as treatments that fall under the broad umbrella of behavior therapy, including traditional behavioral interventions, cognitive–behavioral therapy (CBT), and the more recently developed acceptance- and mindfulness-based behavior therapies. For the most part, behavioral treatments have been found to be among the most efficacious treatments in well-controlled studies, and they have also been found to be effective in clinical settings in which treatments are provided more naturalistically. In most studies, traditional behavioral strategies (e.g., exposure) are used in combination with cognitive strategies, so in this section we consider a wide range of behavioral treatments, including CBT, which typically includes both cognitive and traditional behavioral techniques.

The Society of Clinical Psychology (Division 12 of the American Psychological Association) maintains a website (http://www.psychology. sunysb.edu/eklonsky-/division12/index.html) that describes evidence-based treatments for a wide range of problems (e.g., biofeedback-based treatments for insomnia, CBT for schizophrenia, emotion-focused therapy for depression). The website also indicates whether each treatment is strongly supported by research, modestly supported by research, or controversial and provides several references and information on how to get trained in each approach. At the time that this book was written, the site described a total of 60 treatments for specific psychological disorders. Thirty-eight of the 40 treatments listed as having strong support and 11 of the 16 treatments listed as having modest support were behavioral (Society of Clinical Psychology, 2010). In other words, the vast majority of evidence-based treatments reviewed by the Society of Clinical Psychology appear to fall under the umbrella of behavior therapy, including exposure-based treatments, cognitive interventions, behavioral family treatments, problem-solving training, biofeedback, and other strategies for changing behavior, broadly defined.

One recent article reviewed 16 well-conducted meta-analyses of treatment studies on CBT (Butler, Chapman, Forman, & Beck, 2006). This article reviewed only studies that included cognitive or cognitive–behavioral strategies and did not include studies based only on traditional behavioral treatments (although many of the cognitive–behavioral treatments reviewed in this article included traditional behavioral techniques as part of the treatment). This review considered 16 meta-analyses that included 9,995 participants across 332 studies. These studies included 562 comparisons covering 16 disorders or populations, including anxiety disorders, mood disorders, schizophrenia, relationship problems, anger, bulimia, sexual offending, chronic pain, and child internalizing disorders (e.g., depression, anxiety). The review confirmed what countless individual studies had previously shown: CBT is an effective treatment for a wide range of psychological problems.

Studies have also evaluated the cost-effectiveness of behavioral treatments. One recent article reviewed 22 health economic studies on CBT for anxiety, mood, psychotic, and somatoform disorders (Myhr & Payne, 2006). Evidence from studies conducted in the United States, Canada, United Kingdom, Australia, and Germany has suggested that CBT (provided on its own or in combination with pharmacotherapy) leads to symptom improvements that are well worth the costs. In fact, the cost savings that are realized through reduced use of health care services generally cover the costs directly associated with CBT.

With so many studies demonstrating the positive effects of behavioral treatments, a full review of studies is beyond the scope of this book. Comprehensive reviews of the evidence supporting various behavioral approaches are available elsewhere (e.g., Nathan & Gorman, 2007; O'Donohue & Fisher, 2009). In this section, we provide some examples of meta-analytic studies on behavioral treatments for a selection of common psychological problems: depression, anxiety disorders, and schizophrenia.

Meta-analysis refers to the use of statistical techniques to summarize and integrate results of multiple studies, which can lead to more precise estimates of the effects of a particular intervention than any one individual study (Nestoriuc, Kriston, & Rief, 2010). Although meta-analyses are a very helpful way to synthesize findings from a large number of studies, results are greatly influenced by the quality of the studies included, the methods used to integrate the studies, and a variety of other potential biases and limitations. As a result, findings from meta-analytic studies should be interpreted with caution, just as one should be cautious in interpreting the results of any study (Nestoriuc et al., 2010; Zwahlen, Renehan, & Egger, 2008).

Depression

A wide range of behavioral approaches have been found to be effective for improving mood or reducing rates of relapse in people with major depressive disorder (Craighead, Sheets, Brosse, & Ilardi, 2007). Examples of evidence-based treatments for depression include behavioral activation, problem-solving therapy, social skills training, self-control therapy, behavioral marital therapy, mindfulness-based approaches, and CBTs, which include various combinations of cognitive and behavioral techniques.

Behavioral activation for depression (a treatment involving teaching individuals with depression to increase their activity levels) has been evaluated in at least 34 randomized controlled studies, and two recent meta-analyses concluded that behavioral activation is a well-established treatment for depression that works as well as other established approaches, such as cognitive therapy (Cuijpers, van Straten, & Warmerdam, 2007; Mazzucchelli, Kane, & Rees, 2009). Another meta-analysis, by Ekers, Richards, and Gilbody (2008), concluded that behavioral interventions were more effective for depression than supportive psychotherapy or brief psychotherapy and equally as effective as CBT. A meta-analysis on problem-solving therapy found that this treatment was as effective as other psychotherapies and medication treatments for depression and more effective that various control conditions (Bell & D'Zurilla, 2009).

Behavioral treatments are also effective for reducing relapse rates in depression. A recent meta-analysis by Vittengl, Clark, Dunn, and Jarrett (2007) reviewed 28 studies (with a total of 1,880 participants) on the use of CBT for preventing recurrence of depression. Of those who did not receive continued treatment beyond a standard course of acute CBT, 29% of CBT responders relapsed within 1 year and 54% relapsed within 2 years—rates that are typical of other evidence-based psychotherapies, although lower than those often seen on discontinuation of medication after acute treatment. However, when CBT was continued beyond the standard acute treatment phase, a 21% decrease in relapse during the CBT continuation phase and a 29% reduction in relapse during follow-up were observed. Generally, extending the duration of CBT was more effective than other continued treatments, including medications.

We should note that CBTs are not the only evidence-based psychological treatments for depression. In a recent meta-analysis, Cuijpers, van Straten, Andersson, and van Oppen (2008) examined the results of 53 comparative outcome studies to assess the effects of seven major psychological treatments for mild to moderate depression, including CBT, nondirective supportive psychotherapy, behavioral activation, psychodynamic psychotherapy, problem-solving therapy, interpersonal psychotherapy, and social skills training. Generally, all treatments were about equally effective, except that interpersonal psychotherapy was somewhat more efficacious than the other approaches and nondirective psychotherapy was somewhat less efficacious than the other therapies. However, another study published by the same group found that previous meta-analytic studies may have overestimated the effects of psychotherapy for depression by including too many studies of lower quality, in which psychotherapy tends to have stronger effects (Cuijpers, van Straten, Bohlmeijer, Hollon, & Andersson, 2010). In addition, although interpersonal psychotherapy was found to be somewhat more effective for mild to moderate depression (Cuijpers et al., 2008), a recent study comparing interpersonal psychotherapy with CBT found that CBT was more effective for severe depression (Luty et al., 2007).

In addition to meta-analyses supporting the use of behavioral and cognitive–behavioral therapies for depression in adults, behavioral treatments have been found to have significant (although modest) effects on the treatment of depression in children and adolescents (Klein, Jacobs, & Reinecke, 2007; Weisz, McCarty, & Valeri, 2006). Behavioral interventions are also effective for reducing depression in older adults, particularly for treatments that include seven to 12 sessions (Pinquart, Duberstein, & Lyness, 2007).

Finally, evidence has supported CBT, group psychoeducation, and behavioral family therapy in treating bipolar disorder. In all cases, psychological treatments are used in combination with pharmacotherapy. Behavioral treatments appear to be useful for helping people with bipolar disorder reduce their risk of relapse and recurrence (Beynon, Soares-Weiser, Woolacott, Duffy, & Geddes, 2008; Miklowitz & Craighead, 2007).

Anxiety Disorders

The effectiveness of behavioral strategies for treating anxiety disorders is well established (Antony & Stein, 2009). Behavioral techniques have been used effectively for treating anxiety disorders, either alone (e.g., exposure therapy for specific phobias) or in various combinations (e.g., exposure and cognitive therapy for social anxiety disorder). Strategies that are effective for treating various anxiety disorders include exposure, response prevention, cognitive restructuring, relaxation training, mindfulness- and acceptance-based approaches, and social skills training, to name a few.

Hofmann and Smits (2008) identified 1,165 studies in a review of studies on CBT for anxiety disorders. Of these, only 27 met inclusion criteria for their meta-analysis. They concluded that CBT is an effective treatment for anxiety disorders. However, their conclusion is tempered by a caveat that many individuals respond only partially to CBT, and some do not respond at all. Although no other treatment has been found to be more effective than CBT for treating anxiety disorders, considerable room for improvement remains. Findings from this study confirm those from other meta-analyses (e.g., Norton & Price, 2007) showing that CBT is effective for treating a wide range of anxiety disorders. Even in effectiveness studies that evaluate the effects of treatment in less controlled, real-world settings, CBT is a well-supported psychological treatment for anxiety disorders (Stewart & Chambless, 2009).

In addition to being effective in general adult samples, CBT also appears to be useful for treating anxiety disorders in older adults (Hendriks, Voshaar, Oude, Keijsers, Hoogduin, & van Balkom, 2008) and children (In-Albon & Schneider, 2006). Studies have also supported the use of Internet- and computer-based cognitive–behavioral treatments for anxiety disorders (e.g., Reger & Gahm, 2009).

Finally, in addition to some of the larger meta-analyses evaluating CBT across all anxiety disorders, numerous meta-analyses have supported the use of behavioral approaches for specific anxiety disorders, including panic disorder (e.g., Mitte, 2005; Sánchez-Meca, Rosa-Alcázar, Marín-Martínez, & Gómez-Conesa, 2010), social anxiety disorder (e.g., Federoff & Taylor, 2001), obsessive–compulsive disorder (e.g., Rosa-Alcázar, Sánchez-Meca, Gómez-Conesa, & Marín-Martínez, 2008), posttraumatic stress disorder (e.g., Bisson et al., 2007), generalized anxiety disorder (e.g., Covin, Ouimet, Seeds, & Dozois, 2008), and specific phobia (Wolitzky-Taylor, Horowitz, Powers, & Telch, 2008).

Schizophrenia

A number of behavioral treatments have been found to be useful for treating schizophrenia, although always in combination with pharmacotherapy. In a meta-analysis of 22 studies, social skills training led to moderate improvements in social and daily living skills, community functioning, and negative symptoms among individuals with schizophrenia (Kurtz & Mueser, 2008). In recent years, cognitive–behavioral treatments have been developed to directly target positive symptoms, such as delusional beliefs. CBT appears to have small- to medium-size effects on positive symptoms, as well as on mood and general functioning (Wykes, Steel, Everitt, & Tarrier, 2007). In addition, effect sizes appear to be elevated in studies with methodological limitations, such as those that make no attempt to mask group allocation (Wykes et al., 2007). Finally, evidence from meta-analyses also supports the use of cognitive remediation and psychoeducational coping-oriented interventions with families (Pfammatter, Junghan, & Brenner, 2006).

Conclusion

In addition to studies on depression, anxiety disorders, and schizophrenia, controlled outcome studies have supported the use of behavioral strategies for a wide range of issues, including child conduct disorder (Kazdin, 2007), substance use disorders (Dutra et al., 2008; Powers, Vedel, & Emmelkamp, 2008), insomnia (Moul, Morin, Buysse, Reynolds, & Kupfer, 2007), eating disorders (G. T. Wilson & Fairburn, 2007), effective parenting (de Graaf, Speetjens, Smit, de Wolff, & Tavecchio, 2008); and for various health concerns, such as tension headache (e.g., Nestoriuc, Rief, & Martin, 2008), chronic pain in elderly people (Lunde, Nordhus, & Pallesen, 2009), and child weight loss (Young, Northern, Lister, Drummond, & O'Brien, 2007). In fact, there are few problems for which behavioral therapies have not been found to bring at least some relief.

LIMITATIONS OF BEHAVIOR THERAPY

In general, behavioral treatments have been found to be effective for many psychological problems and in a wide range of populations, including individuals from different age groups and from different cultural and ethnic backgrounds. Nevertheless, many clients make only partial gains after behavioral treatment, and some clients obtain no benefit at all. That is not to say that another form of psychotherapy would necessarily be more effective for these clients. Many of the same factors that predict outcome after behavioral treatments are likely to affect outcome for other treatments as well, although in general there has been relatively little research on non-behavioral psychotherapies for most specific psychological problems.

Outcomes after behavior therapy can be affected by a range of client-related factors and variables related to the therapist and the therapy process (for a review, see Antony, Ledley, & Heimberg, 2005). For example, in CBT for panic disorder, symptom severity, comorbid personality disorders, comorbid depression, quality of the therapeutic relationship, motivation for treatment, and compliance with between-session assignments have all been found to predict treatment outcome (McCabe & Antony, 2005). However, the relationships between these variables and treatment efficacy are often modest, and studies often have inconsistent results.

In addition, a client's expectancies regarding therapy may affect treatment outcome (Westra, Dozois, & Marcus, 2007), suggesting that an individual who has a strong preference for a treatment other than behavior therapy may be less likely to benefit from behavioral treatment. Beliefs and expectancies may also predict relapse and recurrence after treatment. For example, in a double-blind study of individuals being treated for panic disorder with agoraphobia with a combination of psychological treatment (either exposure or relaxation training) and medication (either alprazolam or placebo), Başoğlu et al. (1994) found that expectations and beliefs were correlated with long-term outcome. Specifically, the extent to which patients believed that their gains were because of the medication (regardless of whether they took alprazolam or placebo) rather than psychological treatment was correlated with their tendency to experience withdrawal symptoms and worsening during the 6-month follow-up phase. Individuals who believed that their improvements were related to their psychological treatment (rather than medication) were less likely to experience a worsening of symptoms during follow-up, after they had discontinued their medication and behavioral treatment.

Related to client expectancies, motivation and compliance can also affect treatment outcome. Behavior therapy is an active intervention that requires clients to invest considerable time and energy into the therapy process. Poor motivation and a lack of compliance with between-session assignments can negatively affect the results of therapy. For individuals who are ambivalent about treatment, it may be useful to integrate strategies for enhancing motivation, such as motivational interviewing, which is a client-centered intervention designed to help clients resolve ambivalence and enhance motivation. Motivational interviewing has been found to enhance outcomes in cognitive–behavioral treatments for a number of psychological problems (Arkowitz et al., 2008).

Behavioral treatments may need to be adapted, depending on the specific client (Federici, Rowa, & Antony, 2010). For example, treatment for developmentally disabled individuals who lack the intellectual ability to use certain strategies effectively may need to focus on strategies that rely less on complex techniques such as cognitive restructuring and self-monitoring forms (e.g., Klein-Tasman & Albano, 2007). Very little research has been conducted on treating most psychological disorders (e.g., anxiety disorders, depression) in the context of low cognitive or intellectual functioning, although strategies based on operant conditioning are well established for helping individuals with developmental disabilities manage specific problem behaviors.

There may also be cases in which administering behavioral treatments in the standard way is potentially dangerous. For example, although exposure to driving is the treatment of choice for most people who fear driving, standard exposure therapy might not be appropriate for an individual who tends to become extremely dizzy while driving. In these cases, exposure would likely occur much more gradually (to minimize dizziness) or might be avoided altogether in favor of other strategies, such as cognitive restructuring, relaxation training, or medication. Exposure in virtual reality might also be beneficial in a case like this.

Similarly, although most individuals with OCD who experience sexual obsessions do not pose any risk, some individuals may have features of both OCD and pedophilia in that they become sexually aroused in response to their intrusive thoughts about children. For most clients with OCD who experience unwanted sexual obsessions involving children, exposure to situations and intrusive thoughts involving children is an appropriate treatment. However, if an individual is aroused when experiencing inappropriate sexual thoughts about children (even if he or she is also distressed by the thoughts), exposure would likely be contraindicated, and another evidence-based treatment (e.g., pharmacotherapy) would be preferred. Before initiating behavioral treatments with a particular client, issues related to safety and potential ethical concerns need to be considered.

Finally, it is important to note that limitations sometimes observed in behavioral treatments may not reflect inadequacies of the behavioral model but rather a lack of skill and experience in the specific therapist. The success of behavior therapy depends on an accurate functional analysis, selection of appropriate target behaviors and reinforcers, and selection of appropriate interventions. Ensuring that therapists have adequate training is key to the success of behavioral treatments.

EFFICACY WITH CLIENTS FROM DIVERSE BACKGROUNDS

As with all forms of therapy, the empirical basis for using behavior therapies with clients who identify with any of a range of minority or marginalized statuses is woefully inadequate. Fortunately, increasing attention to the need for attention to cultural factors in therapy has led to several useful resources to guide clinicians in providing behavioral or cognitive–behavioral therapies with clients from diverse backgrounds (e.g., Hays & Iwamasa, 2006, for culturally responsive CBT; and Martell, Safren, & Prince, 2004, for CBTs with lesbian, gay, and bisexual clients), as well as more general guides for culturally responsive practice (e.g., Hays, 2007; Sue, 2006).

The few randomized controlled trials of behavior therapy or CBT that have been conducted with clients from ethnic or racial minority backgrounds have provided preliminary support for the efficacy of this approach. For instance, a few studies have suggested that CBTs may be efficacious in the treatment of depression among Latino and Latina adults and youth, although improvements are often smaller in magnitude than in trials with predominantly White clients (for a review, see Organista, 2006). A randomized controlled trial of group panic control treatment with African American women revealed significant symptomatic improvements among individuals who received the treatment (Carter, Sbrocco, Gore, Marin, & Lewis, 2003). A culturally adapted CBT for Cambodian refugees with treatment-resistant posttraumatic stress disorder and panic attacks led to significant improvements in a broad range of symptoms in an initial randomized controlled trial (Hinton et al., 2005).

In the absence of a well-developed body of empirical research to offer guidance in the use of behavior therapies with clients from diverse backgrounds, therapists need to attend to the theoretical and empirical research on therapy with individuals from specific backgrounds, a review of which is beyond the scope of this book, as well as to theory and research on behavioral principles, to provide culturally competent and responsive behavioral therapy. As Hays (2006) noted, an important first step is to engage in the ongoing process of increasing one's knowledge of and experience with specific cultural groups, to reveal the culturally based biases that may undermine one's ability to work effectively and respectfully with individuals from specific backgrounds. The books cited earlier provide useful initial steps and guidance in this important process. An attitude of humility and awareness of the areas of ignorance, inexperience, and bias that all therapists have is important in this process.

Behavioral approaches have some inherent strengths that may aid in the process of using them in culturally responsive treatment. The emphasis on environmental causal factors and the underlying assumption that all behaviors are functional in a specific context provide a framework that allows for a conceptualization of a client's presenting problems in her or his cultural context. Functional analysis allows for an exploration of the ways in which contextual factors can contribute to mental health difficulties among members of many oppressed groups. This approach may also minimize the stigma often associated with mental health difficulties in specific cultural groups because a functional analysis can illustrate the ways in which emotions and behaviors relate to context and learning history rather than reflect individual weaknesses. Nonetheless, a culturally informed behavior therapist needs to expand the typical targets of assessment to include culturally relevant factors, including values and conceptualizations of mental health issues, sources of healing and support, and the client's own cultural identification or acculturative status, as well as that of the client's family. In addition, therapists need to attend to the real barriers that may exist in a client's life because of discrimination and systemic inequalities, language abilities, financial strain, and other environmental factors. Often, behavioral theories overlook real environmental constraints, which invalidates clients' experiences and may minimize the ability to promote change. Tanaka-Matsumi, Seiden, and Lam (1996) provided a useful model for a culturally informed functional assessment, and Okazaki and Tanaka-Matsumi (2006) discussed cultural considerations in assessment more broadly.

Another potential strength of a behavioral approach is the emphasis on a collaborative therapeutic relationship in which the client is seen as the expert on his or her own experience. The development of a collaborative conceptualization and treatment plan necessitates consideration of the client's cultural background and views that may play a role in goals for therapy and the optimal means for achieving these goals. Nonetheless, behavior therapists need to attend to the power imbalance inherent in the therapeutic relationship, which may mirror systemic inequalities if the therapist identifies with a dominant culture in relation to the client. Moreover, when clients and therapists come from differing backgrounds, there may be added challenges to developing a collaborative relationship. Therapists need to attend to these challenges and work to make sure that a client feels her or his lived experience is fully understood and considered throughout treatment. This may involve repeatedly revising the conceptualization and treatment plan to find a shared perspective that allows therapy to move forward productively. In addition, behavior theory grew out of a Western tradition and reflects inherent Western values, such as an emphasis on individual, as opposed to collective, goals and well-being, as well as on scientific inquiry as opposed to models of faith or spirituality. Therapists must be careful not to impose these values on clients and to instead allow clients' own values to guide the goals and course of therapy. For clients for whom family connections and interdependent views of self are salient, it may be helpful to involve family members in therapy. In addition, the emphasis on valued living in acceptance and commitment therapy and other acceptance-based behavioral therapies may be one way to ensure that clients' values, rather than therapists' values, shape therapy (Lee, Fuchs, Roemer, & Orsillo, 2009). Attention to cultural strengths and sources of healing and support can help identify culturally congruent paths toward behavior change (Hays, 2006).

Another potential strength of behavioral approaches is the focus on thoughts as serving a function, like any behavior, but not necessarily playing a causal role in responses (in contrast to cognitive models). Although cognitive therapists run the risk of responding to culturally based beliefs as "irrational" or trying to challenge these beliefs, possibly alienating clients and weakening the therapeutic alliance, behavior therapists would naturally focus more on helping a client identify ways to respond optimally in contexts, regardless of the thoughts that arise. Nonetheless, sensitivity to culturally based beliefs and the potential for these beliefs to play an important role in behavior change is essential. In addition, therapists need to attend to their own potential biases in what they consider "optimal" functioning and be sure that their goals are congruent with their clients' goals.

Behavior therapists also need to attend to their clients' contexts in considering between-session assignments and practice. Typical behavioral protocols assume that clients can spend a great deal of time at home engaging in the tasks of therapy, with minimal interruption, which may not correspond to the lived experience of many clients. Attending to the function of these planned assignments (e.g., noticing thoughts and cues that elicit particular responses, developing skills such as relaxation or mindfulness) can guide therapists as they adapt assignments to conform to their clients' actual lives. Briefer practices, including more informal practices while engaging in other tasks (e.g., diaphragmatic breathing while attending to household tasks, practicing mindfulness while sitting on the bus), and briefer monitoring strategies (e.g., checking off observations rather than writing them out, recording observations once a day, recalling situations in the context of therapy instead of monitoring between sessions) can help clients gain the skills and perspective that assignments are aimed to enhance while still fitting realistically into the complexities of clients' lives.

The preceding comments are only a very brief introduction to considerations that arise in providing behavior therapies to clients from a range of backgrounds in terms of race, ethnicity, class, age, sexual orientation, or other salient identities. As with therapies of all orientations, therapists should be sure to follow multicultural guidelines for effective practice.

6

Future Developments

Given their strong basis in empirical study, behavior therapies are likely to keep evolving as research continues to provide guidelines for their refinement and expansion. Here we highlight some important areas of current and future study.

USING BASIC RESEARCH TO IDENTIFY FACTORS THAT FACILITATE NEW LEARNING

Consistent with its history of drawing from basic research in deriving behavioral principles that can be applied to psychotherapy, new developments in behavior therapy are drawing from experimental research to identify potential ways of enhancing new learning (i.e., extinction learning). A potentially promising new area of study involves the use of D-cycloserine (DCS; a partial N-methyl-D-aspartate receptor agonist) to facilitate exposure therapies for anxiety disorders (Norberg, Krystal, & Tolin, 2008). Animal research has found that injections of DCS enhance extinction of fear learning, leading clinical researchers to explore the use of DCS in exposure-based therapies.

A meta-analysis of animal and human findings (Norberg et al., 2008) found that DCS was associated with a significant, large effect size, compared with placebo, in facilitating fear extinction during exposure. Effects were larger in animal than in human studies, and in human studies, effects were larger in clinical than in nonclinical samples. DCS has been found to facilitate exposure therapy in studies of specific phobia, social phobia, panic, and obsessive–compulsive disorder; Norberg et al. (2008) noted that studies with more complex disorders such as posttraumatic stress disorder are needed. They concluded that DCS seems to be most effective when administered shortly before or just after an extinction or exposure trial and that it may make exposure therapy more efficient. More research is needed to determine the optimal dosage and timing of administration, as well as to assess the maintenance of gains, although studies that included follow-up have provided preliminary evidence of sustained gains.

In addition to continued study of the utility of DCS in augmenting the effects of exposure-based therapies, more research is needed to identify the conditions that maximize learning and its generalizability. Craske et al. (2008) provided a detailed description of a number of promising strategies (including DCS) that might enhance learning, drawing from existing experimental research. For instance, they suggested that including multiple conditioned stimuli in exposures and deliberately heightening the mismatch with clients' expectancies for the occurrence of aversive events may enhance the learning of nonfearful associations. They also suggested that the presence of retrieval cues during exposure trials that will be present in new contexts may reduce the likelihood that fearful associations return when the context changes. Studies of these and other strategies in human clinical samples are needed. Behavior therapists and researchers should also continue to draw from neuroscience findings in examining the mechanisms of emotional learning to inform treatment development.

ROLE OF VALUES CLARIFICATION AND VALUED ACTION IN BEHAVIOR THERAPIES

The development of acceptance-based behavior therapies has led to a number of studies investigating the effects of mindfulness and acceptance on a range of outcomes. This research should continue, with an increased focus on the contexts in which these strategies have beneficial consequences, the optimal methods for cultivating these skills, and the mechanisms underlying any demonstrated effects. However, another component of acceptance-based behavior therapies, valued action (which has been the most deeply developed and discussed in the context of acceptance and commitment therapy, e.g., K. G. Wilson & Murrell, 2004; K. G. Wilson, Sandoz, Flynn, Slater, & DuFrene, 2010) has received considerably less empirical attention.

On one hand, an emphasis on helping clients to live the lives they want to be living has been an implicit part of behavior therapies from the beginning. For instance, behavior therapies that address clients' social anxiety inevitably increase clients' engagement with people who matter to them and their ability to meet new people, whereas therapies that reduce excessive drinking undoubtedly improve the quality of their relationships. In addition, the presenting problems that are targeted in behavior therapies, such as anxiety or depression, may be acting as obstacles to valued living, and their reduction may naturally lead to an increase in meaningful actions, without specifically targeting this domain.

On the other hand, a focus on what is meaningful to the client, and attention to clarifying what is most important to her or him, may provide an important motivation for engaging in challenging activities such as exposure to feared contexts or increasing behavioral activation. And, consistent with the theoretical underpinnings of acceptance and commitment therapy, clients may benefit from turning their attention away from efforts to alter their internal experiences and toward focusing directly on living the life they want to be living. A small body of experimental research has seemed to suggest that even engaging with one's values for a brief writing exercise can enhance positive emotions, reduce cortisol in response to stress, and even improve academic performance (for a review of this literature, see K. G. Wilson et al., 2010).

Considerably more research is needed to determine whether an emphasis on valued living enhances behavior therapies. As Arch and Craske (2008) noted, it will be important to directly examine whether an emphasis on values enhances motivation to engage in therapy. In addition, they noted that more research is needed on the relationship between symptom reduction and engagement in valued living, as either may be argued to lead to the other. Moreover, examining broader outcomes such as quality of life in important domains of living will be important for determining whether an emphasis on values has effects beyond those typically assessed in outcome studies (i.e., symptom reduction).

If an emphasis on values is found to enhance treatment, then it will be important to determine optimal methods for clarifying values with clients, as well as strategies for enhancing valued action. Wilson's work in this area (K. G. Wilson & Murrell, 2004; K. G. Wilson et al., in press), as well as that of others (Roemer & Orsillo, 2009), will provide a good starting point for refining and testing methods for identifying and exploring what is most important to clients and helping them to engage in valued actions more frequently and consistently.

PRINCIPLES AND MECHANISMS OF CHANGE

Although randomized controlled trials have helped to identify efficacious treatment packages based in behavioral principles, research is needed to determine which elements of these complex treatments are efficacious and the mechanisms underlying this efficacy so that treatments can be more effectively adapted in practice. Recognition of this need has led to suggestions to move from identifying empirically supported treatments to empirically supported principles of therapeutic change (Castonguay & Beutler, 2006; Rosen & Davison, 2003). This shift in emphasis would allow for precise identification of mechanisms of change that could then be explicitly targeted in treatment, potentially leading to more efficient and focused interventions.

Identification of efficacious elements and mechanisms of change underlying these elements may also help to resolve ongoing debates such as the utility of cognitive versus behavioral strategies or acceptance-based behavioral therapies versus cognitive behavioral therapies (CBTs). As noted earlier, these disparate techniques may operate through similar principles. Alternatively, these techniques may represent different pathways that are more likely to be efficacious with some individuals than with others. These will be important questions for research to address in the coming years.

Studies are also needed that carefully examine the therapist, client, and relationship factors that might facilitate change in behavior therapies. Such studies should address how these factors may interact with one another to provide clinicians with guidance on how best to promote change for specific clients. As noted earlier, these factors have historically been underemphasized in behavioral research, yet existing research has suggested that they play an important role and warrant further investigation.

PROCESS OF THERAPEUTIC CHANGE

Another understudied area in behavior therapies is the process of therapeutic change. Process research is more common in the context of other theoretical orientations. However, given the emphasis on using continued assessments to guide therapist decision making, developing an improved understanding of the course of change in behavioral treatments is needed. Such research will help to identify indicators of new learning, as well as indicators of obstructions to new learning. Therapists could then use these indicators to determine whether to continue with a treatment plan or to choose a different therapeutic strategy because the current plan is not yielding any indication of progress.

An excellent example of the kind of research needed is Hayes and colleagues' research on the nonlinear, dynamic, variable pattern of change in psychotherapy (e.g., A. M. Hayes, Feldman, Beevers, Laurenceau, & Cardaciotto, 2007; A. M. Hayes, Laurenceau, Feldman, Strauss, & Cardaciotto, 2007). A. M. Hayes, Laurenceau, et al. (2007) proposed that change in psychotherapy may follow a nonlinear pattern because, ideally, clients are moving from a fixed, stable system in which problematic behaviors are habitual and predictable to a new fixed, stable system in which new, adaptive behaviors become habitual and predictable. Change may therefore involve a period of variability and instability as clients move from one fixed system to the next. Initial findings have suggested that a temporary worsening of symptoms may predict positive outcomes for at least some clients being treated with a CBT for depression (Hayes, Feldman, et al., 2007). More research of this type will help behavior therapists to determine whether a worsening of symptoms suggests that the process of change has begun or that a different treatment approach should be considered.

CULTURAL ADAPTATIONS

Although behavior therapies are promising in the treatment of people from diverse backgrounds for the reasons reviewed earlier, a better understanding is needed of how best to adapt behavioral therapies to work with people from different backgrounds and how to attend to salient cultural factors and considerations in these applications. It will also be important to learn more about how to adapt treatments so that they are less time and resource intensive and so that they can be used with clients with fewer resources who may not be able to comply with the level of homework that typically characterizes behavior therapies.

Such research should address cultural adaptations that would enhance the applicability of behavioral strategies to the lived experience of people from specific backgrounds. In addition, attention should be paid to how best to effectively establish and maintain a collaborative, supportive therapeutic relationship when the therapist and client differ in cultural background. Research that specifically explores ways to adapt behavioral principles to address racism-related stress and other psychological consequences of discrimination will also be important.

Qualitative studies will be needed in this area of research to better capture the complexities of cultural identification and to avoid the imposition of dominant cultural values on participants who identify with marginalized cultural identities. Qualitative approaches would allow for treatment development efforts to emerge from the experiences of clients from specific backgrounds, incorporating cultural resources and healing practices. Such studies could also assess clients' responses to and expectancies for therapy. An improved understanding of how clients from specific backgrounds respond to therapy, coupled with increased attention to factors that enhance the therapeutic alliance as previously noted, could help to address the well-documented low use of mental health services and high rates of dropout among individuals from many specific cultural groups (Sue, 1998; Wang et al., 2005).

EFFECTIVENESS, PORTABILITY, AND TRAINING ISSUES

An extremely important recent development in treatment research has been a focus on examining the effectiveness of behavior therapies by conducting studies directly in clinics and examining whether behavioral interventions yield similar effects outside the context of carefully controlled randomized controlled trials, which are typically characterized by intensive supervision and a more narrow range of clients. Initial findings of effectiveness are promising; a recent meta-analysis of effectiveness studies of CBTs for anxiety disorders found large effect sizes that were generally comparable with effect sizes from representative efficacy studies (Stewart & Chambless, 2009).

More research is needed on how to adapt the behavior therapies that have been developed in randomized controlled trials to meet the realities of clinical care. Challenges in these adaptations include comorbid, complex clinical presentations; insurance-imposed constraints on number of sessions; frequency of missed sessions; and a modal therapy length of a single session. Identification of principles of change will help in the development of more flexible treatments that can be adapted to varying lengths on the basis of the clinical context's constraints. Careful functional analysis can help with prioritizing treatment targets for individuals with comorbid clinical presentations so that treatment is likely to target multiple presenting problems. Research is also needed to identify ways of enhancing engagement in treatment (e.g., Swartz et al., 2007; drawing from writings on motivational interviewing [Miller & Rollnick, 2002] and culturally responsive therapy [Hays, 2007]) so that clients receive a sufficient dose of treatment.

More work is also needed to determine what constitutes a sufficient dose of therapy. Recently, researchers have begun to explore the utility of stepped-care models in which less intensive interventions (e.g., psychoeducation, bibliotherapy) are provided initially and gradually more intensive interventions are offered to individuals who fail to respond to the initial interventions. Tolin, Diefenbach, Maltby, and Hannan (2005) described a pilot study in which a stepped-care approach to treating obsessive–compulsive disorder revealed promising results in terms of cost-effectiveness, with a subset of clients responding to earlier phases of treatment. Computerized or computer-aided CBT has also been proposed as a way to aid in dissemination and cost-effectiveness of cognitive behavioral interventions. Although some programs have demonstrated efficacy (for a review, see Green & Iverson, 2009), more research is needed to determine the effectiveness of these interventions with a range of presenting problems. As Green and Iverson (2009) noted, such interventions may be efficacious in a stepped-care approach that allows for more therapist contact when clients need it. In this way, clients who are ambivalent about treatment, or on a waiting list, might begin with computerized behavior therapies. Increased access (e.g., for clients in areas in which there are fewer available therapists or with clients who have difficulty attending regularly scheduled sessions) is one potential advantage of computerized interventions that is worthy of further investigation (Green & Iverson, 2009).

Another important consideration in the portability of behavioral treatments to clinical contexts is identifying the optimal methods for training therapists in behavioral principles. The proliferation of behavior therapy manuals (and the computerized versions of behavior therapy described earlier) may lead to the impression that these treatments can be conducted by simply following a treatment manual that was developed for a clinical trial. However, as we have attempted to demonstrate in this book, a clear understanding of behavioral principles is an essential component of conducting behavior therapies because this understanding underlies all clinical decision making and allows for flexibility and responsiveness to the client's specific responses. Studies of the most efficient ways of teaching behavioral principles and their application will help to facilitate high-quality training of clinicians so that they can provide flexible behavior therapy, informed by behavioral principles and existing research.

7

Summary

Behavior therapy is not a unified approach to treatment. Rather, behavior therapy is both varied and changing, and therapists differ with respect to their theoretical assumptions and the strategies they use in treatment. The focus of behavior therapy is on changing behavior, including overt behavioral responses (e.g., avoiding feared situations) and internal behavioral responses (e.g., cognitions, physiological responses). Behavior therapy views all behavior as having a function, and interventions are aimed at changing variables that currently maintain problem behavior. It is directive and active, and behavioral treatments are supported by more research than any other psychological treatment and for a wide range of psychological disorders.

HISTORY

Behavior therapy was first established as a school of psychotherapy around the middle of the 20th century and was influenced by both a proliferation of experimental research and theory related to learning processes and a dissatisfaction with psychoanalysis, the most popular approach to therapy at that time. It is rooted firmly in learning theory, including classical conditional paradigms (e.g., the work of Ivan Pavlov and John Watson) and operant conditioning paradigms (e.g., the work of Edward Thorndike and B. F. Skinner). Behavior therapy emerged simultaneously in South Africa (e.g., the development of exposure-based treatment for fear by Joseph Wolpe, Arnold Lazarus, and Stanley Rachman), the United Kingdom (e.g., early behavior therapy research by Hans Eysenck, Cyril Franks, Stanley Rachman, Isaac Marks, and others at London's Maudsley Hospital), and North America (e.g., Nathan Azrin and Teodoro Ayllon's early work on token economy and other reinforcement-based approaches).

In 1955, Albert Ellis started to combine cognitive strategies with traditional behavioral approaches to develop what would be the first formalized system of cognitive–behavioral therapy (CBT). Through the 1960s and 1970s, a number of prominent researchers (e.g., Aaron Beck, Gerald Davison, Marvin Goldfried, Michael Mahoney, Donald Meichenbaum, and Walter Mischel) further developed cognitive techniques, and today CBT is the most frequently practiced form of behavior therapy. In recent years, a third wave of behavior therapy has emerged, with an emphasis on the importance of acceptance as a strategy for dealing with unwanted thoughts, emotions, and physical feelings, as well as the importance of living a life that is consistent with one's values.

THEORY

From a behavioral perspective, clinical problems are learned. These habitual, stuck patterns of responding have developed over time as a result of associations and contingencies in the environment (which can also include the internal environment, e.g., physical sensations, thoughts, imagery) that maintain these patterns in a given context. Behavior therapy aims to identify the factors that currently maintain the difficulties in question and to intervene to reduce problematic behaviors and responses and increase more flexible, adaptive behaviors and responses. Stuck patterns of responding can be learned through association (e.g., when a person comes to fear a cue because it was paired with something dangerous), consequence (e.g., when a behavior such as drinking is negatively reinforced by a reduction in negative affect), modeling (e.g., when a parent models a tendency to respond to frustration with violence), and verbal learning (e.g., when a child learns to avoid expressing emotions after a caregiver expresses the view that showing emotions is a sign of weakness). Cues and contingencies serve to maintain problematic behaviors. By identifying the function a behavior serves and its maintaining factors, therapist and client can work to promote new learning and reduce problematic responding. Broad, flexible patterns of responding, in contrast to habitual, rigid patterns of responding, are expected to respond to current environmental contingencies and context and therefore to be more adaptive and promote optimal functioning.

PROCESS: PRIMARY CHANGE MECHANISMS

Behavioral assessment has a number of goals, including developing a better understanding of a client's problems (from a behavioral perspective); describing the presence, absence, or severity of particular symptoms; making inferences about the causes of a client's problems (especially environmental influences); predicting future behavior; developing appropriate treatments; and measuring treatment outcome. Behaviors of interest are measured throughout treatment so that strategies can be changed as needed. Behavioral assessment also relies on multiple informants (e.g., client, family members, teachers) and multiple methods, including behavioral interviews, functional analysis, behavioral observation, self-monitoring, standard self-report scales, and psychophysiological measures. Relative to other forms of assessment, behavioral assessment is idiographic, focusing on the assessment of behavioral antecedents, target behaviors, and consequences that are unique to a given individual.

Commonly used techniques of behavior therapy include psychoeducation, exposure (e.g., to feared situations, objects, thoughts, images, and feelings), response prevention (e.g., stopping safety behaviors and compulsive rituals), behavioral activation for depression, strategies based on operant conditioning, cognitive strategies, modeling, relaxation-based strategies, biofeedback, mindfulness- and acceptance-based strategies,

emotion regulation skills training, social and communication skills training, problem-solving training, stimulus control procedures, and strategies
for preventing relapse.

Although research and practice in behavior therapy have tended to
focus most on the effects of behavioral techniques, the importance of the
therapeutic relationship and therapy process in behavioral treatment is
increasingly recognized. Therapist factors that have been identified
as potentially related to treatment outcome include empathy, positive
regard, congruence and genuineness, and self-disclosure. From a behavioral perspective, these characteristics may promote change because they
reinforce desired behaviors, provide experiences that challenge interpersonal expectancies, provide models of adaptive interpersonal behavior, promote engagement in therapy and collaboration on treatment
goals, and facilitate emotional engagement. The therapeutic relationship
has also received considerable attention in the research literature. The
working alliance is associated with outcome in behavioral treatments,
especially when the alliance is reported by clients rather than therapists.
Furthermore, working alliance ratings in CBT have generally been found
to be comparable or stronger than working alliance ratings in insight-
oriented or psychodynamic therapies. Although client factors have
received less research attention than therapist factors and the therapeutic
relationship, a client's motivation for treatment, compliance with treatment
procedures, and openness to discussing problems may affect the outcome
of behavior therapy.

Perhaps the biggest challenge in behavior therapy has been a difficulty
in disseminating behavioral treatments to practicing clinicians and ensuring that these interventions are available for those who need them. One
problem is that there are too many different evidence-based behavioral
protocols, and there is no way that any one clinician can learn more than
a handful of these treatments. In addition, many clinicians have been
reluctant to adopt evidence-based treatments such as behavior therapy
because of misunderstandings about the underlying principles of behavioral treatment, assumptions that behavioral treatments will not work for
their clients, contextual or institutional factors, and a lack of training in
behavior therapy. The most commonly reported barrier to adopting

evidence-based treatments is training, suggesting that more attention needs to be paid to training issues if evidence-based treatments such as behavior therapy are to be widely adopted.

EVALUATION

No psychotherapy has been subjected to as much research as behavior therapy, including traditional behavioral interventions, CBT, and more recently developed acceptance- and mindfulness-based behavioral therapies. For the most part, behavioral treatments have been found to be among the most efficacious treatments in well-controlled studies, and they have also been found to be effective in naturalistic clinical settings. Controlled treatment studies have supported the use of behavioral and cognitive–behavioral treatments for anger, anxiety disorders, bipolar disorder, child internalizing disorders, chronic pain, conduct disorder, depression, eating disorders, insomnia, parent training, relationship problems, schizophrenia, sexual offending, substance use disorders, weight loss, and various other problems.

Despite the benefits of behavior therapy, many clients obtain only partial gains after behavioral treatment, and some clients do not benefit at all. Outcome can be affected by therapist skill and experience, the quality of the therapeutic relationship, client motivation, comorbidity, client expectancies, and a number of other factors. Recently, there has been an increase in research on methods of adapting behavior therapy for clients who are less likely to benefit from behavioral treatments as they are usually administered. An example would be CBT adapted for a particular cultural or ethnic minority group. Although research on behavioral treatments for clients from diverse backgrounds is woefully inadequate, emerging evidence has suggested that behavior therapy and CBTs are effective for clients from a range of ethnic and racial backgrounds, ages, and other diverse groups, especially when therapists pay attention to cultural, developmental, and other contextual factors and incorporate these considerations into their conceptualization and treatment of presenting problems.

SUGGESTIONS FOR FUTURE DEVELOPMENT

Given their strong basis in empirical evidence, behavior therapies are likely to keep evolving as research continues to provide guidelines for their refinement and expansion. Several areas of development are currently underway. Cultural adaptations of behavior therapies and examination of their efficacy and effectiveness will be extremely important to ensure culturally responsible care. More research is also needed to identify principles and mechanisms of change and to increase understanding of the process of therapeutic change. Developments in these areas will help to improve the portability of behavior therapy and to optimize training in provision of behavior therapies, so that more people can benefit from behavioral approaches to change. Basic research is also needed to improve understanding of factors that enhance the acquisition and maintenance of new learning, so interventions can be improved on the basis of this knowledge. Moreover, research that examines the process of values clarification and increases in valued action will help to ensure that treatments more effectively help clients to live meaningful lives—an ultimate goal of psychotherapy.

Glossary of Key Terms

ABSTINENCE VIOLATION EFFECT   A term used in relapse prevention to describe the phenomenon in which an individual may give up all behavior change efforts after a lapse because his or her abstinence has been violated.

ACCEPTANCE AND COMMITMENT THERAPY   An acceptance-based behavior therapy developed by Steven Hayes and colleagues that emphasizes the importance of acceptance as a strategy for dealing with unwanted thoughts and feelings, as well as the importance of living a life that is consistent with one's values.

ACCEPTANCE-BASED BEHAVIOR THERAPIES   Also sometimes referred to as "third-wave" behavior therapies, refers to a group of behavior therapies that incorporate an emphasis on acceptance of, rather than efforts to suppress or avoid, internal experiences.

APPLIED BEHAVIOR ANALYSIS   The extension of B. F. Skinner's principles of operant conditioning to applied settings, such as schools and hospitals, and settings in which psychotherapy is provided.

AVERSIVE CONDITIONING   The pairing of a behavior with an aversive consequence (or punishment).

BEHAVIORAL ACTIVATION   A behavioral treatment for depression that was developed by Neil Jacobson and colleagues and involves increasing activity levels in a client's day-to-day life that are likely to lead to reinforcement from the environment.

BEHAVIORAL EXPERIMENT   A strategy used in cognitive therapy in which a client engages in some activity for the purpose of testing the accuracy of a specific belief.

BEHAVIORISM   An approach to psychology founded by John Watson that emphasizes observable behaviors and objective facts rather than subjective experiences such as cognition, emotion, and motivation.

CLASSICAL CONDITIONING   A process of learning through association. Previously neutral stimuli that are paired with stimuli that naturally evoke certain responses will come to be associated with the stimuli with which they have co-occurred and will evoke related responses.

COGNITIVE–BEHAVIORAL THERAPY   A form of psychotherapy that integrates learning theory and cognitive theory and that includes both cognitive and behavioral strategies.

COGNITIVE RESTRUCTURING   A technique used in cognitive–behavioral therapy in which clients identify, refute, and change self-defeating beliefs and predictions so they are more reasonable and adaptive.

COGNITIVE THERAPY   An approach to therapy developed by Aaron Beck that focuses on teaching clients to identify and change maladaptive beliefs and assumptions.

CONDITIONED STIMULUS   A previously neutral stimulus that, because of its prior association with a stimulus that naturally evokes a response, comes to elicit a conditioned response.

COVERT SENSITIZATION   A punishment-based procedure in which a client imagines performing an undesired behavior, followed by imagining an unwanted consequence.

D-CYCLOSERINE   A partial agonist of the N-methyl-D-aspartate receptor that has been found to enhance learning during exposure therapy and thereby leads to improved outcomes.

DIALECTICAL BEHAVIOR THERAPY   Developed by Marsha Linehan for the treatment of borderline personality disorder; includes a variety of behavioral, cognitive, and mindfulness-based strategies.

DISCRIMINANT STIMULUS   A stimulus in the environment that indicates that a given behavior may be reinforced.

DISULFIRAM   A drug that causes nausea, vomiting, and symptoms of physiological arousal when combined with alcohol and that is sometimes used in the aversive treatment of alcohol abuse and dependence.

EXPOSURE HIERARCHY   A list of feared situations rank ordered from the most frightening (at the top) to the least frightening (at the bottom), used to guide practices in exposure therapy.

EXPOSURE THERAPY   A treatment that involves confronting feared situations, objects, thoughts, images, or physical sensations until they are no longer frightening.

FUNCTIONAL ANALYSIS   The process of identifying what precedes and what follows (i.e., antecedents and consequences) clinically relevant behaviors to determine how they are maintained.

HIGHER ORDER CONDITIONING   The process through which a previously neutral stimulus becomes associated with a conditioned stimulus with which it is paired, so that learned associations spread.

IMAGINAL EXPOSURE   Confronting a feared stimulus in imagination until it is no longer frightening.

INHIBITORY LEARNING (EXTINCTION)   The process through which inhibitory associations are developed to a conditioned stimulus because it is presented in the absence of the unconditioned stimulus, leading to new learning that counters the initial conditioned associations.

INTEROCEPTIVE EXPOSURE   Confronting feared physical sensations by completing exercises that trigger the sensations (e.g., spinning to trigger dizziness) until they are no longer frightening.

IN VIVO EXPOSURE   Confronting a feared stimulus live and in person (as opposed to in imagination) until it is no longer frightening.

LAW OF EFFECT   The principle that the consequences of behavior affect the probability of the behavior's occurring again in the future.

META-ANALYSIS   A statistical procedure for synthesizing the results of a large number of studies to provide a single estimate of the combined effect found across the studies.

MINDFULNESS   A process that involves cultivating nonjudgmental awareness of the present moment and is an integral part of many acceptance-based behavior therapies.

MODELING   A process of learning through observation or imitation that is sometimes included in behavior therapy.

MOTIVATIONAL INTERVIEWING   An approach developed by William Miller and Stephen Rollnick that uses client-centered, semidirective methods to increase clients' motivation to change behavior.

NEGATIVE REINFORCEMENT   The removal of something an individual finds aversive, which increases the frequency of a target behavior.

OPERANT LEARNING   The process of learning through consequences, with some consequences (reinforcers) increasing the frequency of behaviors and others (punishers) decreasing the frequency of behaviors.

POSITIVE REINFORCEMENT   The presentation of something an individual finds desirable, which increases the frequency of a target behavior.

PREMACK PRINCIPLE   Engaging in a high-frequency behavior after a lower frequency behavior to increase the frequency of (i.e., reinforce) the first behavior.

PROGRESSIVE MUSCLE RELAXATION   Tensing and relaxing various muscle groups to become more aware of feelings of tension and learning to relax the muscles of the body.

PUNISHER   A consequence that decreases the frequency of the preceding behavior.

RADICAL BEHAVIORISM   The view that behavior should be the focus of psychological science, with an emphasis on the environmental determinants of behavior (e.g., reinforcement, punishment).

RATIONAL EMOTIVE BEHAVOR THERAPY   A form of cognitive–behavioral therapy developed by Albert Ellis, previously known as *rational therapy* and *rational emotive therapy.*

RECIPROCAL INHIBITION   A technique used to substitute an undesired response with a desired one through counterconditioning or substitute a response that is incompatible with the original one (see systematic desensitization).

RULE-GOVERNED LEARNING   Behaviors that are learned through instruction rather than through direct experience.

SOCIAL REINFORCER   A reinforcer that is socially mediated, such as expressions of praise or approval.

STIMULUS CONTROL   The extent to which behavior is influenced by particular stimuli.

STIMULUS GENERALIZATION   When a classically conditioned association to a particular conditioned stimulus extends to other, similar stimuli so that conditioned responses occur to a broader range of stimuli.

SYSTEMATIC DESENSITIZATION   A treatment developed by Joseph Wolpe that pairs graduated imaginal exposure to a feared object or situation with progressive muscle relaxation.

TARGET BEHAVIOR   A behavior that has been selected for modification during behavior therapy.

TIME OUT   A technique in which an undesired behavior is decreased by removing the individual from the area in which the behavior had previously been reinforced.

TOKEN ECONOMY   A technique in which desired behaviors are reinforced by giving an individual tokens that can be exchanged for rewards.

UNCONDITIONED STIMULUS   A stimulus that naturally evokes certain responses.

VALUES CLARIFICATION   The process of helping a client identify what is truly important to her or him. It is an integral part of acceptance and commitment therapy and other acceptance-based behavioral approaches.

WORKING ALLIANCE   The quality and strength of the collaborative relationship between the therapist and the client (i.e., affective bond, agreement on goals and tasks).

Suggested Readings

HISTORICAL AND THEORETICAL PERSPECTIVES IN BEHAVIOR THERAPY

Kazantzis, N., Reinecke, M. A., & Freeman, A. (Eds.). (2010). *Cognitive and behavioral theories in clinical practice.* New York, NY: Guilford Press.

Kazdin, A. E. (1978). *History of behavior modification.* Baltimore, MD: University Park Press.

O'Donohue, W. T., Henderson, D. A., Hayes, S. C., Fisher, J. E., & Hayes, L. J. (Eds.). (2001). *A history of the behavior therapies: Founders personal histories.* Reno, NV: Context Press.

O'Donohue, W., & Krasner, L. (Eds.). (1995). *Theories of behavior therapy: Exploring behavior change.* Washington, DC: American Psychological Association.

Plaud, J. J., & Eifert, G. H. (1998). *From behavior theory to behavior therapy.* Boston, MA: Allyn & Bacon.

BEHAVIORAL ASSESSMENT

Haynes, S. N., & Heiby, E. M. (Eds.). (2004). *Comprehensive handbook of psychological assessment: Vol. 3. Behavioral assessment.* Hoboken, NJ: Wiley.

Haynes, S. N., & O'Brien, W. O. (2000). *Principles and practice of behavioral assessment.* New York, NY: Springer.

Nelson, R. O., & Hayes, S. C. (1986). *Conceptual foundations of behavioral assessment.* New York, NY: Guilford Press.

CONTEMPORARY BEHAVIORAL THERAPIES

Abramowitz, J. S., Deacon, B. J., & Whiteside, S. P. (2011). *Exposure therapy for anxiety: Principles and practice.* New York, NY: Guilford Press.

Antony, M. M., Ledley, D. R., & Heimberg, R.G. (Eds.). (2005). *Improving outcomes and preventing relapse in cognitive behavioral therapy.* New York, NY: Guilford Press.

Arkowitz, H., Westra, H. A., Miller, W. R., & Rollnick, S. (2008). *Motivational interviewing in the treatment of psychological problems.* New York, NY: Guilford Press.

Barlow, D. H. (Ed.). (2008). *Clinical handbook of psychological disorders: A step-by-step treatment manual* (4th ed.). New York, NY: Guilford Press.

Bernstein, D. A., Borkovec, T. D., & Hazlett-Stevens, H. (2000). *New directions in progressive relaxation training: A guidebook for helping professionals.* Westport, CT: Praeger.

Bieling, P. J., McCabe, R. E., & Antony, M. M. (2006). *Cognitive behavioral therapy in groups.* New York, NY: Guilford Press.

Craske, M. G. (2010). *Cognitive–behavioral therapy.* Washington, DC: American Psychological Association.

Dobson, D., & Dobson, K. S. (2009). *Evidence-based practice of cognitive–behavioral therapy.* New York, NY: Guilford Press.

Dobson, K. S. (Ed.). (2010). *Handbook of cognitive–behavioral therapies* (2nd ed.). New York, NY: Guilford Press.

Hayes, S. C., Strosahl, K. D., & Wilson, K. G. (1999). *Acceptance and commitment therapy: An experiential approach to behavior change.* New York, NY: Guilford Press.

Hersen, M., & Rosqvist, J. (Eds.). (2005). *Encyclopedia of behavior modification and cognitive behavior therapy: Vol. 1. Adult clinical applications.* Thousand Oaks, CA: Sage.

Kazantzis, N., Reinecke, M. A., & Freeman, A. (2010). *Cognitive and behavioral theories in clinical practice.* New York, NY: Guilford Press.

Miller, W. R., & Rollnick, S. (2002). *Motivational interviewing: Preparing people for change* (2nd ed.). New York, NY: Guilford Press.

O'Donohue, W. T., & Fisher, J. E. (Eds.). (2009). *Cognitive behavior therapy: Applying empirically supported techniques in your practice* (2nd ed.). Hoboken, NJ: Wiley.

O'Donohue, W. T., & Fisher, J. E. (Eds.). (2009). *General principles and empirically supported techniques of cognitive behavior therapy.* Hoboken, NJ: Wiley.

Richard, D. C. S., & Lauterbach, D. (2007). *Handbook of exposure therapies.* New York, NY: Academic Press.

Roemer, L., & Orsillo, S. M. (2009). *Mindfulness- and acceptance-based behavioral therapies in practice.* New York, NY: Guilford Press.

Spiegler, M. D., & Guevremont, D. C. (2010). *Contemporary behavior therapy* (5th ed.). Belmont, CA: Wadsworth.

Wright, J. H., Basco, M. R., & Thase, M. E. (2006). *Learning cognitive–behavior therapy: An illustrated guide.* Washington, DC: American Psychiatric Press.

CLASSICS IN BEHAVIOR THERAPY

Bandura, A. (1969). *Principles of behavior modification.* New York, NY: Holt, Rinehart & Winston.

Bandura, A., & Walters, R. H. (1963). *Social learning and personality development.* New York, NY: Holt, Rinehart & Winston.

Eysenck, H. J. (Ed.). (1964). *Experiments in behaviour therapy.* London, England: Pergamon Press.

Franks, C. M. (Ed.). (1969). *Behavior therapy: Appraisal and status.* New York, NY: McGraw-Hill.

Goldfried, M. R., & Davison, G. C. (1994). *Clinical behavior therapy* (Expanded ed.). New York, NY: Wiley Interscience.

Kanfer, F. H., & Goldstein, A. P. (Eds.). (1991). *Helping people change: A textbook of methods* (4th ed.). New York, NY: Pergamon Press.

Kanfer, F. H., & Phillips, J. S. (1970). *Learning foundations of behavior therapy.* New York, NY: Wiley.

Krasner, L., & Ullman, L. P. (Eds.). (1965). *Research in behavior modification.* New York, NY: Holt, Rinehart & Winston.

Mahoney, M. J. (1974). *Cognition and behaviour modification.* Cambridge, MA: Ballinger.

Paul, G. L. (1966). *Insight versus desensitization in psychotherapy.* Stanford, CA: Stanford University Press.

Ullmann, L. P., & Krasner, L. (Eds.). (1965). *Case studies in behavioral modification.* New York, NY: Holt, Rinehart & Winston.

Wolpe, J. (1958). *Psychotherapy by reciprocal inhibition.* Stanford, CA: Stanford University Press.

Wolpe, J. (1969). *The practice of behavior therapy.* New York, NY: Pergamon Press.

Wolpe, J., & Lazarus, A. A. (1966). *Behavior therapy techniques.* Oxford, England: Pergamon Press.

References

Abramowitz, J. S. (2009). *Getting over OCD: A 10-step workbook for taking back your life.* New York, NY: Guilford Press.

Abramowitz, J. S., Deacon, B. J., & Whiteside, S. P. H. (2011). *Exposure therapy for anxiety: Principles and practice.* New York, NY: Guilford Press.

Allen, L. B., McHugh, R. K., & Barlow, D. H. (2008). Emotional disorders: A unified protocol. In D. H. Barlow (Ed.), *Clinical handbook of psychological disorders: A step-by-step treatment manual* (4th ed., pp. 216–249). New York, NY: Guilford Press.

American Psychiatric Association. (2000). *Diagnostic and statistical manual of mental disorders* (4th ed., text revision). Washington, DC: Author.

American Psychiatric Association. (2007). *Practice guideline for the treatment of patients with obsessive–compulsive disorder.* Arlington, VA: Author. Retrieved from http://www.psychiatryonline.com/pracGuide/pracGuideTopic_10.aspx

Amir, N., Beard, C., Burns, M., & Bomyea, J. (2009). Attention modification program in individuals with generalized anxiety disorder. *Journal of Abnormal Psychology, 118,* 28–33. doi:10.1037/a0012589

Antony, M. M., Ledley, D. R., & Heimberg, R. G. (Eds.). (2005). *Improving outcomes and preventing relapse in cognitive behavioral therapy.* New York, NY: Guilford Press.

Antony, M. M., & McCabe, R. E. (2004). *10 simple solutions to panic: How to overcome panic attacks, calm physical symptoms, and reclaim your life.* Oakland, CA: New Harbinger.

Antony, M. M., & McCabe, R. E. (2005). *Overcoming animal and insect phobias: How to conquer fear of dogs, snakes, rodents, bees, spiders, and more.* Oakland, CA: New Harbinger.

Antony, M. M., & Norton, P. J. (2009). *The anti-anxiety workbook: Proven strategies to overcome worry, panic, phobias, and obsessions.* New York, NY: Guilford Press.

Antony, M. M., Orsillo, S. M., & Roemer, L. (Eds.). (2001). *Practitioner's guide to empirically based measures of anxiety.* New York, NY: Springer.

Antony, M. M., & Rowa, K. (2008). *Social anxiety disorder: Psychological approaches to assessment and treatment.* Göttingen, Germany: Hogrefe.

Antony, M. M., & Stein, M. B. (Eds.). (2009). *Oxford handbook of anxiety and related disorders.* New York, NY: Oxford University Press.

Antony, M. M., & Swinson, R. P. (2000). *Phobic disorders and panic in adults: A guide to assessment and treatment.* Washington, DC: American Psychological Association. doi:10.1037/10348-000

Antony, M. M., & Watling, M. A. (2006). *Overcoming medical phobias: How to conquer fear of blood, needles, doctors, and dentists.* Oakland, CA: New Harbinger.

Arch, J. J., & Craske, M. G. (2008). Acceptance and commitment therapy and cognitive behavioral therapy for anxiety disorders: Different treatments, same mechanisms? *Clinical Psychology: Science and Practice, 15,* 263–279. doi:10.1111/j.1468-2850.2008.00137.x

Arkowitz, H., Westra, H. A., Miller, W. R., & Rollnick, S. (2008). *Motivational interviewing in the treatment of psychological problems.* New York, NY: Guilford Press.

Ayllon, T. (1963). Intensive treatment of psychotic behavior by stimulus satiation and food reinforcement. *Behaviour Research and Therapy, 1,* 53–61. doi:10.1016/0005-7967(63)90008-1

Ayllon, T., & Azrin, N. H. (1965). The measurement and reinforcement of behavior of psychotics. *Journal of the Experimental Analysis of Behavior, 8,* 357–383. doi:10.1901/jeab.1965.8-357

Ayllon, T., & Azrin, N. H. (1968). *The token economy: A motivational system for therapy and rehabilitation.* New York, NY: Appleton-Century-Crofts.

Bandura, A. (1965). Influence of models' reinforcement contingencies on the acquisition of imitative responses. *Journal of Personality and Social Psychology, 1,* 589–595. doi:10.1037/h0022070

Bandura, A. (1969). *Principles of behavior modification.* New York, NY: Holt, Rinehart & Winston.

Bandura, A. (1977a). Self-efficacy theory: Toward a unifying theory of behavioral change. *Psychological Review, 84,* 191–215. doi:10.1037/0033-295X.84.2.191

Bandura, A. (1977b). *Social learning theory.* Englewood Cliffs, NJ: Prentice Hall.

Bandura, A. (1986). *Social foundations of thought and action: A social cognitive theory.* Englewood Cliffs, NJ: Freeman.

Barlow, D. H., Allen, L. B., & Choate, M. L. (2004). Towards a unified treatment for emotional disorders. *Behavior Therapy, 35,* 205–230. doi:10.1016/S0005-7894(04)80036-4

Barlow, D. H., & Craske, M. G. (2007). *Mastery of your anxiety and panic: Workbook* (4th ed.). New York, NY: Oxford University Press.

Başoğlu, M., Marks, I. M., Swinson, R. P., Noshirvani, H., O'Sullivan, G., & Kuch, K. (1994). Pre-treatment predictors of treatment outcome in panic disorder and agoraphobia treated with alprazolam and exposure. *Journal of Affective Disorders, 30,* 123–132. doi:10.1016/0165-0327(94)90040-X

Beck, A. T. (1976). *Cognitive therapy and the emotional disorders.* New York, NY: Penguin.

Beck, A. T. (1993). Cognitive therapy: Nature and relation to behavior therapy. *Journal of Psychotherapy Practice and Research, 2,* 345–356.

Beck, A. T., Rush, A. J., Shaw, B. F., & Emery, G. (1979). *Cognitive therapy of depression.* New York, NY: Guilford Press.

Becker, C. B., Zayfert, C., & Anderson, E. (2004). A survey of psychologists' attitudes towards and utilization of exposure therapy for PTSD. *Behaviour Research and Therapy, 42,* 277–292. doi:10.1016/S0005-7967(03)00138-4

Bell, A. C., & D'Zurilla, T. J. (2009). Problem-solving therapy for depression: A meta-analysis. *Clinical Psychology Review, 29,* 348–353. doi:10.1016/j.cpr.2009.02.003

Bellack, A. S., & Hersen, M. (Eds.). (1985). *Dictionary of behavior therapy techniques.* New York, NY: Pergamon Press.

Bellack, A. S., Mueser, K. T., Gingerich, S., & Agresta, J. (1997). *Social skills training for schizophrenia.* New York, NY: Guilford Press.

Benjamin, L. T., & Baker, D. B. (Eds.). (2000). History of psychology: The Boulder conference [Special section]. *American Psychologist, 55,* 233–254. doi:10.1037/h0087859

Bernstein, D. A., Borkovec, T. D., & Hazlett-Stevens, H. (2000). *New directions in progressive relaxation training: A guidebook for helping professionals.* Westport, CT: Praeger.

Beynon, S., Soares-Weiser, K., Woolacott, N., Duffy, S., & Geddes, J. R. (2008). Psychosocial interventions for the prevention of relapse in bipolar disorder: Systematic review of controlled trials. *The British Journal of Psychiatry, 192,* 5–11. doi:10.1192/bjp.bp.107.037887

Bisson, J. I., Ehlers, A., Matthews, R., Pilling, S., Richards, D., & Turner, S. (2007). Psychological treatments for chronic post-traumatic stress disorder: Systematic review and meta-analysis. *The British Journal of Psychiatry, 190,* 97–104. doi:10.1192/bjp.bp.106.021402

Bloch, I. (1908). *The sexual life of our time.* New York, NY: Rebman.

Borkovec, T. D., Newman, M. G., Pincus, A., & Lytle, R. (2002). A component analysis of cognitive–behavioral therapy for generalized anxiety disorder and the role of interpersonal problems. *Journal of Consulting and Clinical Psychology, 70,* 288–298. doi:10.1037/0022-006X.70.2.288

Bouton, M. E., Mineka, S., & Barlow, D. H. (2001). A modern learning theory perspective on the etiology of panic disorder. *Psychological Review, 108,* 4–32. doi:10.1037/0033-295X.108.1.4

Bouton, M. E., Woods, A. M., Moody, E. W., Sunshay, C., & García-Gutiérrez, A. (2006). Counteracting the context-dependence of extinction: Relapse and tests of some relapse prevention methods. In M. G. Craske, D. Hermans, & D. Vansteenwegen (Eds.), *Fear and learning: From basic processes to clinical implications* (pp. 175–196). Washington, DC: American Psychological Association. doi:10.1037/11474-009

Butcher, J. N., Graham, J. R., Ben-Porath, Y. S., Tellegen, A., Dahlstrom, W. G., & Kraemmer, B. (2001). *Minnesota Multiphasic Personality Inventory—2 (MMPI–2): Manual for administration and scoring.* Minneapolis: University of Minnesota Press.

Butler, A. C., Chapman, J. E., Forman, E. M., & Beck, A. T. (2006). The empirical status of cognitive-behavioral therapy: A review of meta-analyses. *Clinical Psychology Review, 26,* 17–31. doi:10.1016/j.cpr.2005.07.003

Carter, M. M., Sbrocco, T., Gore, K. L., Marin, N. W., & Lewis, K. L. (2003). Cognitive–behavioral group therapy versus a wait-list control in the treatment of African American women with panic disorder. *Cognitive Therapy and Research, 27,* 505–518. doi:10.1023/A:1026350903639

Castonguay, L. G., & Beutler, L. E. (Eds.). (2006). *Principles of therapeutic change that work.* New York, NY: Oxford University Press.

Chambless, D. L., Baker, M. J., Baucom, D. H., Beutler, L. E., Calhoun, K. S., Crits-Christoph, P., . . . Woody, S. R. (1998). Update on empirically validated therapies, II. *Clinical Psychologist, 51,* 3–16.

Chambless, D. L., Sanderson, W. C., Shoham, V., Bennett Johnson, S., Pope, K. S., Crits-Christoph, P., . . . McCurry, S. (1996). An update on empirically validated therapies. *Clinical Psychologist, 49,* 5–18.

Chorpita, B. F., & Regan, J. (2009). Dissemination of effective mental health treatment procedures: Maximizing the return on a significant investment. *Behaviour Research and Therapy, 47,* 990–993. doi:10.1016/j.brat.2009.07.002

Christensen, A., Wheeler, J. G., & Jacobson, N. S. (2008). Couple distress. In D. H. Barlow (Ed.), *Clinical handbook of psychological disorders: A step-by-step treatment manual* (4th ed., pp. 662–689). New York, NY: Guilford Press.

Cloitre, M., Koenen, K. C., Cohen, L., & Han, H. (2002). Skills training in affective and interpersonal regulation followed by exposure: A phase-based treatment for PTSD related to childhood abuse. *Journal of Consulting and Clinical Psychology, 70,* 1067–1074. doi:10.1037/0022-006X.70.5.1067

Colom, F., Vieta, E., Sánchez-Moreno, J., Palomino-Otiniano, R., Reinares, M., Goikolea, J., . . . Martínez-Arán, A. (2009). Group psychoeducation for stabilized bipolar disorders: 5-year outcome of a randomized clinical trial. *The British Journal of Psychiatry, 194,* 260–265. doi:10.1192/bjp.bp.107.040485

Cook, J. M., Schnurr, P. P., Biyanova, T., & Coyne, J. C. (2009). Apples don't fall far from the tree: Influences on psychotherapists' adoption and sustained use of new therapies. *Psychiatric Services, 60,* 671–676. doi:10.1176/appi.ps.60.5.671

Cook, M., Mineka, S., Wolkenstein, B., & Laitsch, K. (1985). Observational condition of snake fear in unrelated rhesus monkeys. *Journal of Abnormal Psychology, 94,* 591–610. doi:10.1037/0021-843X.94.4.591

Cordova, J. V. (2001). Acceptance in behavior therapy: Understanding the process of change. *Behavior Analyst, 24,* 213–226.

Covin, R., Ouimet, A. J., Seeds, P. M., & Dozois, D. J. A. (2008). A meta-analysis of CBT for pathological worry among clients with GAD. *Journal of Anxiety Disorders, 22,* 108–116. doi:10.1016/j.janxdis.2007.01.002

Craighead, W. E., Sheets, E. S., Brosse, A. L., & Ilardi, S. S. (2007). Psychosocial treatments for major depressive disorder. In P. E. Nathan & J. M. Gorman (Eds.), *A guide to treatments that work* (3rd ed., pp. 289–307). New York, NY: Oxford University Press.

Craske, M. G. (2010). *Cognitive–behavioral therapy.* Washington, DC: American Psychological Association.

Craske, M. G., & Barlow, D. H. (2008). Panic disorder and agoraphobia. In D. H. Barlow (Ed.), *Clinical handbook of psychological disorders: A step-by-step treatment manual* (4th ed., pp. 1–64). New York, NY: Guilford Press.

Craske, M. G., Kircanski, K., Zelikowsky, M., Mystkowski, J., Chowdry, N., & Baker, A. (2008). Optimizing inhibitory learning during exposure. *Behaviour Research and Therapy, 46,* 5–27. doi:10.1016/j.brat.2007.10.003

Craske, M. G., & Mystkowski, J. L. (2006). Exposure therapy and extinction: Clinical studies. In M. G. Craske, D. Hermans, & D. Vansteenwegen (Eds.), *Fear and learning: From basic processes to clinical implications* (pp. 217–233). Washington, DC: American Psychological Association. doi:10.1037/11474-011

Cuijpers, P., van Straten, A., Andersson, G., & van Oppen, P. (2008). Psychotherapy for depression in adults: A meta-analysis of comparative outcome trials. *Journal of Consulting and Clinical Psychology, 76,* 909–922. doi:10.1037/a0013075

Cuijpers, P., van Straten, A., Bohlmeijer, E., Hollon, S. D., & Andersson, G. (2010). The effects of psychotherapy for adult depression are overestimated: A meta-analysis of study quality and effect strength. *Psychological Medicine, 40,* 211–223. doi:10.1017/S0033291709006114

Cuijpers, P., van Straten, A., & Warmerdam, L. (2007). Behavioral activation treatments for depression: A meta-analysis. *Clinical Psychology Review, 27,* 318–326. doi:10.1016/j.cpr.2006.11.001

Davis, C. M., Yarber, W. L., Bauserman, R., & Schreer, G. (1998). *Handbook of sexuality-related measures.* Thousand Oaks, CA: Sage.

de Graaf, I., Speetjens, P., Smit, F., de Wolff, M., & Tavecchio, L. (2008). Effectiveness of the triple P positive parenting program on behavioral problems in children: A meta-analysis. *Behavior Modification, 32,* 714–735. doi:10.1177/0145445508317134

Derogatis, L. R. (1977). *SCL–90: Administration, scoring, and procedures manual–I for the revised version.* Baltimore, MD: Johns Hopkins University School of Medicine, Clinical Psychometrics Research Unit.

Derogatis, L. R. (1994). *SCL–90–R: Administration, scoring, and procedures manual.* Minneapolis, MN: National Computer Systems.

DeRubeis, R. J., Webb, C. A., Tang, T. Z., & Beck, A. T. (2010). Cognitive therapy. In K. S. Dobson (Ed.), *Handbook of cognitive-behavioral therapies* (3rd ed., pp. 277–316). New York, NY: Guilford Press.

Dimidjian, S., Hollon, S. D., Dobson, K. S., Schmaling, K. B., Kohlenberg, R. J., Addis, M. E., . . . Jacobson, N. S. (2006). Randomized trial of behavioral activation, cognitive therapy, and antidepressant medication in the acute treatment of adults with major depression. *Journal of Consulting and Clinical Psychology, 74,* 658–670. doi:10.1037/0022-006X.74.4.658

Dollard, J., & Miller, N. (1950). *Personality and psychotherapy: An analysis in terms of learning, thinking, and culture.* New York, NY: McGraw-Hill.

Donohue, B. C., & Romero, V. (2005). Token economy. In M. Hersen & J. Rosqvist (Eds.), *Encyclopedia of behavior modification and cognitive behavior therapy: Vol. 1. Adult clinical applications* (pp. 594–596). Thousand Oaks, CA: Sage.

Drossel, C., Garrison-Diehn, C. G., & Fisher, J. E. (2009). Contingency management interventions. In W. T. O'Donohue & J. E. Fisher (Eds.), *General principles and empirically supported techniques of cognitive behavior therapy* (pp. 214–220). Hoboken, NJ: Wiley.

Drossel, C., Rummel, C., & Fisher, J. E. (2009). Assessment and cognitive behavior therapy: Functional analysis as key process. In W. T. O'Donohue & J. E. Fisher (Eds.), *General principles and empirically supported techniques of cognitive behavior therapy* (pp. 15–41). Hoboken, NJ: Wiley.

Durand, V. M. (1991). *Severe behavior problems: A functional communication training approach.* New York, NY: Guilford Press.

Dutra, L., Stathopoulou, G., Basden, S. L., Leyro, T. M., Powers, M. B., & Otto, M. W. (2008). A meta-analytic review of psychosocial interventions for substance use disorders. *The American Journal of Psychiatry, 165,* 179–187. doi:10.1176/appi.ajp.2007.06111851

Ehlers, C. L., Frank, E., & Kupfer, D. J. (1988). Social zeitgebers and biological rhythms: A unified approach to understanding the etiology of depression. *Archives of General Psychiatry, 45,* 948–952.

Ehrenreich, J. T., Goldstein, C. R., Wright, L. R., & Barlow, D. H. (2009). Development of a unified protocol for the treatment of emotional disorders in youth. *Child and Family Behavior Therapy, 31,* 20–37.

Ekers, D., Richards, D., & Gilbody, S. (2008). A meta-analysis of randomized trials of behavioural treatment of depression. *Psychological Medicine, 38,* 611–623. doi:10.1017/S0033291707001614

Elias, M. J., & Clabby, J. F. (1992). *Building social problem-solving skills: Guidelines from a school-based program.* San Francisco, CA: Jossey-Bass.

Ellis, A. (2001). The rise of cognitive behavior therapy. In W. T. O'Donohue, D. A. Henderson, S. C. Hayes, J. E. Fisher, & L. J. Hayes (Eds.), *A history of the behavioral therapies: Founders' personal histories* (pp. 183–194). Reno, NV: Context Press.

Ellis, H. (1936). *Studies in the psychology of sex* (2 vols.). New York, NY: Random House.

Emmelkamp, P. M. G., & Kamphuis, J. H. (2005). Aversive relief. In M. Hersen & J. Rosqvist (Eds.), *Encyclopedia of behavior modification and cognitive behavior therapy: Vol. 1. Adult clinical applications* (pp. 39–40). Thousand Oaks, CA: Sage.

Enoch, M. (2007). Genetics, stress, and risk for addiction. In A. Mustafa (Ed.), *Stress and addiction: Psychological and biological mechanisms* (pp. 127–146). San Diego, CA: Elsevier. doi:10.1016/B978-012370632-4/50009-7

Exner, J. E. (1993). *The Rorschach: A comprehensive system: Vol. 1. Basic foundations.* Hoboken, NJ: Wiley.

Eysenck, H. J. (1959). Learning theory and behavior therapy. *Journal of Mental Science, 105,* 61–75.

Eysenck, H. J. (1960). *Behaviour therapy and the neuroses: Readings in modern methods of treatment derived from learning theory.* New York, NY: Pergamon Press.

Eysenck, H. J. (Ed.). (1964). *Experiments in behaviour therapy: Readings in modern methods of treatment of mental disorders derived from learning theory.* New York, NY: Pergamon Press.

Federici, A., Rowa, K., & Antony, M. M. (2010). Adjusting treatment for partial- or nonresponse to contemporary cognitive-behavioral therapy. In D. McKay, J. Abramowitz, & S. Taylor (Eds.), *Cognitive-behavioral therapy for refractory cases: Turning failure into success* (pp. 11–37). Washington, DC: American Psychological Association.

Fedoroff, I. C., & Taylor, S. (2001). Psychological and pharmacological treatments of social phobia: A meta-analysis. *Journal of Clinical Psychopharmacology, 21,* 311–324. doi:10.1097/00004714-200106000-00011

Ferster, C. B. (1973). A functional analysis of depression. *American Psychologist, 28,* 857–870.

Fischer, J., & Corcoran, K. (2007). *Measures for clinical practice and research: A sourcebook* (4th ed., 2 vols.). New York, NY: Oxford University Press.

Foa, E. B., Huppert, J. D., & Cahill, S. P. (2006). Emotional processing theory: An update. In B. O. Rothbaum (Ed.), *Pathological anxiety: Emotional processing in etiology and treatment* (pp. 3–24). New York, NY: Guilford Press.

Foa, E. B., Jameson, J. S., Turner, R. M., & Payne, L. L. (1980). Massed versus spaced exposure sessions in the treatment of agoraphobia. *Behaviour Research and Therapy, 18,* 333–338. doi:10.1016/0005-7967(80)90092-3

Foa, E. B., & Kozak, M. J. (1986). Emotional processing of fear: Exposure to corrective information. *Psychological Bulletin, 99,* 20–35. doi:10.1037/0033-2909.99.1.20

Forel, A. (1922). *The sexual question.* New York, NY: Physician's & Surgeon's.

Foster, S. L., Laverty-Finch, C., Gizzo, D. P., & Osantowski, J. (1999). Practical issues in self-observation. *Psychological Assessment, 11,* 426–438. doi:10.1037/1040-3590.11.4.426

Franklin, M. E., Jaycox, L. H., & Foa, E. B. (1999). Social skills training. In M. Hersen & A. S. Bellack (Eds.), *Handbook of comparative interventions for adult disorders* (2nd ed., pp. 317–339). Hoboken, NJ: Wiley.

Franks, C. M. (1963). Behavior therapy, the principles of conditioning, and the treatment of the alcoholic. *Quarterly Journal of Studies on Alcohol, 24,* 511–529.

Franks, C. M. (2001). From psychodynamic to behavior therapy: Paradigm shift and personal perspectives. In W. T. O'Donohue, D. A. Henderson, S. C. Hayes, J. E. Fisher, & L. J. Hayes (Eds.), *A history of the behavioral therapies: Founders' personal histories* (pp. 195–206). Reno, NV: Context Press.

Franks, C. M., & Wilson, G. T. (1977). *Annual review of behavior therapy: Theory and practice* (Vol. 5). New York, NY: Brunner/Mazel.

Freud, S. (1950). Turnings in the world of psychoanalytic therapy. In J. Strachey (Ed.), *Collected papers of Sigmund Freud* (Vol. 2, pp. 399–400). London, England: Hogarth and Institute of Psychoanalysis. (Original work published 1919)

Gervitz, R. N. (2007). Psychophysiological perspectives on stress-related and anxiety disorders. In P. M. Lehrer, R. L. Woolfolk, & W. E. Sime (Eds.), *Principles and practices of stress management* (3rd ed., pp. 209–226). New York, NY: Guilford Press.

Gilbert, P., & Leahy, R. L. (Eds.). (2007). *The therapeutic relationship in the cognitive behavioral therapies.* New York, NY: Routledge.

Goldfried, M. R., & Sprafkin, J. N. (1976). Behavioral personality assessment. In J. T. Spence, R. C. Carson, & J. Thibaut (Eds.), *Behavioral approaches to therapy* (pp. 295–321). Morristown, NJ: General Learning Press.

Goodman, W. K., Price, L. H., Rasmussen, S. A., Mazure, C., Delgado, P., Heninger, G. R., & Charney, D. S. (1989). The Yale-Brown Obsessive Compulsive Scale: II. Validity. *Archives of General Psychiatry, 46,* 1012–1016.

Goodman, W. K., Price, L. H., Rasmussen, S. A., Mazure, C., Fleischmann, R. L., Hill, C. L., & Charney, D. S. (1989). The Yale-Brown Obsessive Compulsive Scale: I. Development, use, and reliability. *Archives of General Psychiatry, 46,* 1006–1011.

Gratz, K. L., & Gunderson, J. G. (2006). Preliminary data on an acceptance-based emotion regulation group intervention for deliberate self-harm among women with borderline personality disorder. *Behavior Therapy, 37,* 25–35. doi:10.1016/j.beth.2005.03.002

Gratz, K. L., & Roemer, L. (2004). Multidimensional assessment of emotion regulation and dysregulation: Development, factor structure, and initial validation of the Difficulties in Emotion Regulation Scale. *Journal of Psychopathology and Behavioral Assessment, 26,* 41–54.

Green, K. E., & Iverson, K. M. (2009). Computerized cognitive behavioral therapy in a stepped care model of treatment. *Professional Psychology: Research and Practice, 40,* 96–103. doi:10.1037/a0012847

Greenberger, D., & Padesky, C. A. (1995). *Mind over mood: Change how you feel by changing the way you think.* New York, NY: Guilford Press.

Hayes, A. M., & Feldman, G. (2004). Clarifying the construct of mindfulness in the context of emotion regulation and the process of change in therapy. *Clinical Psychology: Science and Practice, 11,* 255–262. doi:10.1093/clipsy/bph080

Hayes, A. M., Feldman, G. C., Beevers, C. G., Laurenceau, J.-P., & Cardaciotto, L. (2007). Discontinuities and cognitive changes in an exposure-based cognitive therapy for depression. *Journal of Consulting and Clinical Psychology, 75,* 409–421. doi:10.1037/0022-006X.75.3.409

Hayes, A. M., Laurenceau, J.-P., Feldman, G., Strauss, J. L., & Cardaciotto, L. (2007). Change is not always linear: The study of nonlinear and discontinuous patterns of change in psychotherapy. *Clinical Psychology Review, 27,* 715–723. doi:10.1016/j.cpr.2007.01.008

Hayes, S. A., Hope, D. A., VanDyke, M. M., & Heimberg, R. G. (2007). Working alliance for clients with social anxiety disorder: Relationship with session helpfulness and within-session habituation. *Cognitive Behaviour Therapy, 36,* 34–42. doi:10.1080/16506070600947624

Hayes, S. C., Barnes-Holmes, D., & Roche, B. (Eds.). (2001). *Relational frame theory: A post-Skinnerian account of human language and cognition.* New York, NY: Springer.

Hayes, S. C., Follette, V. M., & Linehan, M. M. (2004). *Mindfulness and acceptance: Expanding the cognitive-behavioral tradition.* New York, NY: Guilford Press.

Hayes, S. C., Strosahl, K. D., & Wilson, K. G. (1999). *Acceptance and commitment therapy: An experiential approach to behavior change.* New York, NY: Guilford Press.

Hayes, S. C., Wilson, K. G., Gifford, E. V., Follette, V. M., & Strosahl, K. (1996). Experiential avoidance and behavioral disorders: A functional dimensional approach to diagnosis and treatment. *Journal of Consulting and Clinical Psychology, 64,* 1152–1168. doi:10.1037/0022-006X.64.6.1152

Hayes, S. C., Wilson, K. G., Gifford, E. V., Piasecki, M., Byrd, M., Gregg, J., . . . Gregg, J. (2004). A preliminary trial of twelve-step facilitation and acceptance and commitment therapy with polysubstance-abusing methadone-maintained opium addicts. *Behavior Therapy, 35,* 667–688. doi:10.1016/S0005-7894(04)80014-5

Haynes, S. N. (1986). The design of intervention programs. In R. O. Nelson & S. C. Hayes (Eds.), *Conceptual foundations of behavioral assessment* (pp. 386–429). New York, NY: Guilford Press.

Haynes, S. N., & Heiby, E. M. (Eds.). (2004). Comprehensive handbook of psychological assessment. Vol. 3: Behavioral assessment. Hoboken, NJ: Wiley.

Haynes, S. N., & O'Brien, W. O. (2000). *Principles and practice of behavioral assessment.* New York, NY: Springer.

Hays, P. A. (2006). Introduction: Developing culturally responsive cognitive-behavioral therapies. In P. A. Hays & G. Y. Iwamasa (Eds.), *Culturally responsive cognitive-behavioral therapy: Assessment, practice, and supervision* (pp. 3–20). Washington, DC: American Psychological Association.

Hays, P. A. (2007). *Addressing cultural complexities in practice: Assessment, diagnosis, and therapy* (2nd ed.). Washington, DC: American Psychological Association.

Hays, P. A., & Iwamasa, G. Y. (Eds.). (2006). *Culturally responsive cognitive-behavioral therapy: Assessment, practice, and supervision.* Washington, DC: American Psychological Association. doi:10.1037/11433-000

Hendriks, G. J., Voshaar, R. C. O., Keijsers, G. P. J., Hoogduin, C. A. L., & van Balkom, A. L. J. M. (2008). Cognitive-behavioural therapy for late-life anxiety disorders: A systematic review and meta-analysis. *Acta Psychiatrica Scandinavica, 117,* 403–411. doi:10.1111/j.1600-0447.2008.01190.x

Herbert, J. D., Forman, E. M., & Englund, E. L. (2009). Psychological acceptance. In W. T. O'Donahue & J. E. Fisher (Eds.), *General principles and empirically supported techniques of cognitive behavior therapy* (pp. 102–114). Hoboken, NJ: Wiley.

Hinton, D. E., Chhean, D., Pich, V., Hofmann, S. G., Pollack, M. H., & Safren, S. A. (2005). A randomized controlled trial of cognitive behavior therapy for Cambodian refugees with treatment resistant PTSD and panic attacks: A cross-over design. *Journal of Traumatic Stress, 18,* 617–629. doi:10.1002/jts.20070

Hofmann, S. G., & Smits, J. A. J. (2008). Cognitive-behavioral therapy for adult anxiety disorders: A meta-analysis of randomized placebo-controlled trials. *Journal of Clinical Psychiatry, 69,* 621–632.

Horvath, A. O., & Bedi, R. P. (2002). The alliance. In J. C. Norcross (Ed.), *Psychotherapy relationships that work: Therapist contributions and responsiveness to patients* (pp. 37–69). New York, NY: Oxford University Press.

Hunsley, J., & Mash, E. J. (2010). The role of assessment in evidence-based practice. In M. M. Antony & D. H. Barlow (Eds.), *Handbook of assessment and treatment planning psychological disorders* (2nd ed.; pp. 3–22). New York, NY: Guilford Press.

In-Albon, T., & Schneider, S. (2006). Psychotherapy of childhood anxiety disorders: A meta-analysis. *Psychotherapy and Psychosomatics, 76,* 15–24.

Itard, J. M. G. (1962). *The wild boy of Aveyron.* New York, NY: Meredith.

Jacobson, E. (1938). *Progressive relaxation.* Chicago, IL: University of Chicago Press.

Jacobson, N. S., Dobson, K. S., Truax, P. A., Addis, M. E., Koerner, K., Gollan, J. K., . . . Prince, S. E. (1996). A component analysis of cognitive–behavioral treatment for depression. *Journal of Consulting and Clinical Psychology, 64,* 295–304. doi:10.1037/0022-006X.64.2.295

Jacobson, N. S., Martell, C. R., & Dimidjian, S. (2001). Behavioral activation treatment for depression: Returning to contextual roots. *Clinical Psychology: Science and Practice, 8,* 255–270. doi:10.1093/clipsy/8.3.255

Janet, P. (1925). *Psychological healing: A historical and clinical study.* London, England: Allen & Unwin.

Jones, M. C. (1924). A laboratory study of fear: The case of Peter. *Journal of General Psychology, 31,* 308–315.

Kabat-Zinn, J. (2005). *Coming to our senses: Healing ourselves and the world through mindfulness.* New York, NY: Hyperion.

Kanfer, F. H., & Grimm, L. G. (1977). Behavioral analysis: Selecting target behaviors in the interview. *Behavior Modification, 1,* 7–28. doi:10.1177/014544557711002

Kazdin, A. E. (2007). Psychosocial treatments for conduct disorder in children and adolescents. In P. E. Nathan & J. M. Gorman (Eds.), *A guide to treatments that work* (3rd ed., pp. 71–104). New York, NY: Oxford University Press.

Keijsers, G. P. J., Schaap, C. D. P. R., & Hoogduin, C. A. L. (2000). The impact of interpersonal patient and therapist behavior on outcome in cognitive-behavior therapy: A review of empirical studies. *Behavior Modification, 24,* 264–297. doi:10.1177/0145445500242006

Kelley, M. L., Reitman, D., & Noell, G. H. (2002). *Practitioner's guide to empirically based measures of school behavior.* New York, NY: Springer.

Kenny, W. C., Alvarez, K., Donohue, B. C., & Winick, C. B. (2008). Overview of behavioral assessment with adults. In M. Hersen & J. Rosqvist (Eds.), *Handbook of psychological assessment, case conceptualization, and treatment: Vol. 1. Adults* (pp. 3–25). Hoboken, NJ: Wiley.

Kent, G. (1997). Dental phobias. In G. C. Davey (Ed.), *Phobias: A handbook of theory, research and treatment* (pp. 107–127). Chichester, England: Wiley.

Klein, J. B., Jacobs, R. H., & Reinecke, M. A. (2007). Cognitive-behavioral therapy for adolescent depression: A meta-analytic investigation of changes in effect-size estimates. *Journal of the American Academy of Child and Adolescent Psychiatry, 46,* 1403–1413. doi:10.1097/chi.0b013e3180592aaa

Klein-Tasman, B. P., & Albano, A. M. (2007). Intensive, short-term cognitive behavioral treatment of OCD-like behavior in a young adult with Williams syndrome. *Clinical Case Studies, 6,* 483–492. doi:10.1177/1534650106296370

Kohlenberg, R. J., & Tsai, M. (1995). Functional analytic psychotherapy: A behavioral approach to intensive treatment. In W. O'Donohue & L. Krasner (Eds.), *Theories of behavior therapy* (pp. 637–658). Washington, DC: American Psychological Association. doi:10.1037/10169-023

Kohlenberg, R. J., & Tsai, M. (2007). *Functional analytic psychotherapy: Creating intense and curative therapeutic relationships.* New York, NY: Springer.

Kurtz, M. M., & Mueser, K. T. (2008). A meta-analysis of controlled research on social skills training for schizophrenia. *Journal of Consulting and Clinical Psychology, 76,* 491–504. doi:10.1037/0022-006X.76.3.491

Lang, P. J., Melamed, B. G., & Hart, J. (1970). A psychophysiological analysis of fear modification using an automated desensitization procedure. *Journal of Abnormal Psychology, 76,* 220–234. doi:10.1037/h0029875

La Roche, M. J., D'Angelo, E., Gualdron, L., & Leavell, J. (2006). Culturally sensitive relaxation imagery for allocentric Latinos: A pilot study. *Psychotherapy: Theory, Research, Practice, Training, 43,* 555–560. doi:10.1037/0033-3204.43.4.555

Lawrence, E., Eldridge, K., Christensen, A., & Jacobson, N. S. (1999). Integrative couple therapy: The dyadic relationship of acceptance and change. In J. M. Donovan (Ed.), *Short-term couple therapy* (pp. 226–261). New York, NY: Guilford Press.

Lazarus, A. A. (1958). New methods in psychotherapy: A case study. *South African Medical Journal, 33*, 660–664.

Lazarus, A. A. (2001). A brief personal account of CT (conditioning therapy), BT (behavior therapy), and CBT (cognitive-behavior therapy): Spanning three continents. In W. T. O'Donohue, D. A. Henderson, S. C. Hayes, J. E. Fisher, & L. J. Hayes (Eds.), *A history of the behavioral therapies: Founders' personal histories* (pp. 155–162). Reno, NV: Context Press.

Lee, J. K., Fuchs, C., Roemer, L., & Orsillo, S. M. (2009). Cultural considerations in acceptance-based behavioral therapies. In L. Roemer & S. M. Orsillo (Eds.), *Mindfulness- and acceptance-based behavioral therapies in practice* (pp. 116–118). New York, NY: Guilford Press.

Lejuez, C. W., Hopko, D. R., & Hopko, S. D. (2001). A brief behavioral activation treatment for depression: Treatment manual. *Behavior Modification, 25*, 255–286. doi:10.1177/0145445501252005

Lincoln, T. M., Wilhelm, K., & Nestoriuc, Y. (2007). Effectiveness of psychoeducation for relapse, symptoms, knowledge, adherence and functioning in psychotic disorders: A meta-analysis. *Schizophrenia Research, 96*, 232–245. doi:10.1016/j.schres.2007.07.022

Lindsley, O. R. (2001). Studies in behavior therapy and behavior research laboratory: June 1953–1965. In W. T. O'Donohue, D. A. Henderson, S. C. Hayes, J. E. Fisher, & L. J. Hayes (Eds.), *A history of the behavioral therapies: Founders' personal histories* (pp. 125–153). Reno, NV: Context Press.

Lindsley, O. R., Skinner, B. F., & Solomon, H. C. (1953). *Studies in behavior therapy* (Status Report 1). Waltham, MA: Metropolitan State Hospital.

Linehan, M. M. (1993a). *Cognitive-behavioral treatment for borderline personality disorder.* New York, NY: Guilford Press.

Linehan, M. M. (1993b). *Skills training manual for cognitive behavioral treatment of borderline personality disorder.* New York, NY: Guilford Press.

Linehan, M. M., Comtois, K. A., Murray, A. M., Brown, M. Z., Gallop, R. J., Heard, H. L., Korslund, K. E., . . . Lindenboim, N. (2006). Two-year randomized controlled trial and follow-up of dialectical behavior therapy vs. therapy by experts for suicidal behaviors and borderline personality disorder. *Archives of General Psychiatry, 63*, 757–766. doi:10.1001/archpsyc.63.7.757

Lonsdorf, T. B., Weike, A. I., Nikamo, P., Schalling, M., Hamm, A. O., & Öhmann, A. (2009). Genetic gating of human fear learning and extinction:

Possible implications for gene-environment interaction in anxiety disorders. *Psychological Science, 20,* 198–206. doi:10.1111/j.1467-9280.2009.02280.x

Lunde, L.-H., Nordhus, I. H., & Pallesen, S. (2009). The effectiveness of cognitive and behavioural treatment of chronic pain in the elderly: A quantitative review. *Journal of Clinical Psychology in Medical Settings, 16,* 254–262. doi:10.1007/s10880-009-9162-y

Luty, S. E., Carter, J. D., McKenzie, J. M., Rae, A. M., Frampton, C. M. A., Mulder, R. T., & Joyce, P. R. (2007). Randomised controlled trial of interpersonal psychotherapy and cognitive behavioural therapy for depression. *British Journal of Psychiatry, 190,* 496–502. doi:10.1192/bjp.bp.106.024729

Magee, L., Erwin, B. A., & Heimberg, R. G. (2009). Psychological treatment of social anxiety disorder and specific phobia. In M. M. Antony & M. B. Stein (Eds.), *Oxford handbook of anxiety and related disorders* (pp. 334–349). New York, NY: Oxford University Press.

Marlatt, G. A., & Donovan, D. M. (2005). *Relapse prevention: Maintenance strategies in the treatment of addictive behaviors.* New York, NY: Guilford Press.

Marlatt, G. A., & Gordon, J. R. (Eds.). (1985). *Relapse prevention.* New York, NY: Guilford Press.

Martell, C. R., Addis, M. E., & Jacobson, N. S. (2001). *Depression in context: Strategies for guided action.* New York, NY: Norton.

Martell, C. R., Safren, S. A., & Prince, S. E. (2004). *Cognitive behavioral therapies with lesbian, gay, and bisexual clients.* New York, NY: Guilford Press.

Mazzucchelli, T., Kane, R., & Rees, C. (2009). Behavioral activation treatments for depression in adults: A meta-analysis and review. *Clinical Psychology: Science and Practice, 16,* 383–411. doi:10.1111/j.1468-2850.2009.01178.x

McCabe, R. E., & Antony, M. M. (2005). Panic disorder and agoraphobia. In M. Antony, D. R. Ledley, & R. Heimberg (Eds.), *Improving outcomes and preventing relapse in cognitive behavioral therapy* (pp. 1–37). New York, NY: Guilford Press.

McNally, R. J., & Reese, H. E. (2008). Information-processing approaches to understanding anxiety disorders. In M. M. Antony & M. B. Stein (Eds.), *Oxford handbook of anxiety and related disorders* (pp. 136–152). New York, NY: Oxford University Press.

Mellon, M. W. (2005). Bell and pad bladder training. In A. M. Gross & R. S. Drabman (Eds.), *Encyclopedia of behavior modification and cognitive behavior therapy: Vol. 2. Child clinical applications* (pp. 746–750). Thousand Oaks, CA: Sage.

Mennin, D. S., & Farach, F. (2007). Emotion and evolving treatments for adult psychopathology. *Clinical Psychology: Science and Practice, 14,* 329–352. doi:10.1111/j.1468-2850.2007.00094.x

Mennin, D. S., & Fresco, D. M. (2010). Emotion regulation as an integrative framework for understanding and treating psychopathology. In A. M. Kring & D. M. Sloan (Eds.), *Emotion regulation and psychopathology: A transdiagnostic approach to etiology and treatment* (pp. 356–379). New York, NY: Guilford Press.

Miklowitz, D. J., & Craighead, W. E. (2007). Psychosocial treatments for bipolar disorder. In P. E. Nathan & J. M. Gorman (Eds.), *A guide to treatments that work* (3rd ed., pp. 309–322). New York, NY: Oxford University Press.

Miller, W. R. (1985). Motivation for treatment: A review with special emphasis on alcoholism. *Psychological Bulletin, 98,* 84–107. doi:10.1037/0033-2909.98.1.84

Miller, W. R., & Rollnick, S. (2002). *Motivational interviewing: Preparing people for change* (2nd ed.). New York, NY: Guilford Press.

Mineka, S., & Cook, M. (1986). Immunization against the observational conditioning of snake fear in rhesus monkeys. *Journal of Abnormal Psychology, 95,* 307–318. doi:10.1037/0021-843X.95.4.307

Mineka, S., Gunnar, M., & Champoux, M. (1986). Control and early socioemotional development: Infant rhesus monkeys reared in controllable versus uncontrollable environments. *Child Development, 57,* 1241–1256. doi:10.2307/1130447

Mineka, S., & Zinbarg, R. (2006). A contemporary learning theory perspective on the etiology of anxiety disorders: It's not what you thought it was. *American Psychologist, 61,* 10–26. doi:10.1037/0003-066X.61.1.10

Mitte, K. (2005). A meta-analysis of the efficacy of psycho- and pharmacotherapy in panic disorder with and without agoraphobia. *Journal of Affective Disorders, 88,* 27–45. doi:10.1016/j.jad.2005.05.003

Morin, C. M., Bootzin, R. R., Buysse, D. J., Edinger, J. D., Espie, C. A., & Lichstein, K. L. (2006). Psychological and behavioral treatment of insomnia: Update of the recent evidence (1998–2004). *Sleep, 29,* 1398–1414.

Moscovitch, D. A., Antony, M. M., & Swinson, R. P. (2009). Exposure-based treatments for anxiety disorders: Theory and process. In M. M. Antony & M. B. Stein (Eds.), *Oxford handbook of anxiety and related disorders* (pp. 461–475). New York, NY: Oxford University Press.

Moul, D. E., Morin, C. M., Buysse, D. J., Reynolds, C. F., & Kupfer, D. J. (2007). Treatments for insomnia and restless legs syndrome. In P. E. Nathan & J. M. Gorman (Eds.), *A guide to treatments that work* (3rd ed., pp. 611–640). New York, NY: Oxford University Press.

Mowrer, O. H., & Mowrer, W. M. (1938). Enuresis: A method for its study and treatment. *American Journal of Orthopsychiatry, 8,* 436–459. doi:10.1111/j.1939-0025.1938.tb06395.x

Myhr, G., & Payne, K. (2006). Cost-effectiveness of cognitive-behavioural therapy for mental disorders: Implications for public health care funding policy in Canada. *Canadian Journal of Psychiatry, 51,* 662–670.

Nangle, D. W., Hansen, D. J., Erdley, C. A., & Norton, P. J. (2010). *Practitioner's guide to empirically based measures of social skills.* New York, NY: Springer.

Nathan, P. E., & Gorman, J. M. (Eds.). (2007). *A guide to treatments that work* (3rd ed.). New York, NY: Oxford University Press.

Nelson, R. O. (1988). Relationships between assessment and treatment within a behavioral perspective. *Journal of Psychopathology and Behavioral Assessment, 10,* 155–170. doi:10.1007/BF00962641

Nestoriuc, Y., Kriston, L., & Rief, W. (2010). Meta-analysis as the core of evidence-based behavioral medicine: tools and pitfalls of a statistical approach. *Current Opinion in Psychiatry, 23,* 145–150. doi:10.1097/YCO.0b013e328336666b

Nestoriuc, Y., Rief, W., & Martin, A. (2008). Meta-analysis of biofeedback for tension-type headache: Efficacy, specificity, and treatment moderators. *Journal of Consulting and Clinical Psychology, 76,* 379–396. doi:10.1037/0022-006X.76.3.379

Newring, K. A. B., Loverich, T. M., Harris, C. D., & Wheeler, J. (2009). Relapse prevention. In W. T. O'Donohue & J. E. Fisher (Eds.), *General principles and empirically supported principles of cognitive behavior therapy* (pp. 520–531). Hoboken, NJ: Wiley.

Nezu, A. M. (2004). Problem solving and behavior therapy revisited. *Behavior Therapy, 35,* 1–33. doi:10.1016/S0005-7894(04)80002-9

Nezu, A. M., & Perri, M. G. (1989). Problem-solving therapy for unipolar depression: An initial dismantling investigation. *Journal of Consulting and Clinical Psychology, 57,* 408–413. doi:10.1037/0022-006X.57.3.408

Nezu, A. M., Ronan, G. F., Meadows, E. A., & McClure, K. S. (2000). *Practitioner's guide to empirically based measures of depression.* New York, NY: Springer.

Nock, M. K. (2005). Response prevention. In M. Hersen & J. Rosqvist (Eds.), *Encyclopedia of behavior modification and cognitive behavior therapy: Vol. 1. Adult clinical applications* (pp. 489–493). Thousand Oaks, CA: Sage.

Norberg, M. M., Krystal, J. H., & Tolin, D. F. (2008). A meta-analysis of d-cycloserine and the facilitation of fear extinction and exposure therapy. *Biological Psychiatry, 63,* 1118–1126. doi:10.1016/j.biopsych.2008.01.012

Norcross, J. C. (Ed.). (2002). *Psychotherapy relationships that work: Therapist contributions and responsiveness to patients.* New York, NY: Oxford University Press.

Norton, P. J. P., & Price, E. C. M. A. (2007). A meta-analytic review of adult cognitive-behavioral treatment outcome across the anxiety disorders. *Journal of Nervous and Mental Disease, 195,* 521–531. doi:10.1097/01.nmd.0000253843.70149.9a

O'Brien, W. H., Kaplar, M. E., & Haynes, S. N. (2005). Behavioral assessment. In M. Hersen & J. Rosqvist (Eds.), *Encyclopedia of behavior modification and cognitive behavior therapy: Vol. 1. Adult clinical applications* (pp. 82–90). Thousand Oaks, CA: Sage.

O'Donohue, W. T., & Fisher, J. E. (Eds.). (2009). *General principles and empirically supported techniques of cognitive behavior therapy*. Hoboken, NJ: Wiley.

Okazaki, S., & Tanaka-Matsumi, J. (2006). Cultural consideration in cognitive–behavioral assessment. In P. A. Hays & G. Y. Iwamasa (Eds.), *Culturally responsive cognitive-behavioral therapy: Assessment, practice, and supervision* (pp. 247–266). Washington, DC: American Psychological Association. doi:10.1037/11433-011

Ollendick, T. H., Alvarez, H. K., & Greene, R. W. (2004). Behavioral assessment: History of underlying concepts and methods. In S. N. Haynes & E. M. Heiby (Eds.), *Comprehensive handbook of psychological assessment: Vol. 3. Behavioral assessment*. Hoboken, NJ: Wiley.

Ollendick, T. H., & Grills, A. E. (2005). Modeling. In M. Hersen & J. Rosqvist (Eds.), *Encyclopedia of behavior modification and cognitive behavior therapy: Vol. 1. Adult clinical applications* (pp. 907–910). Thousand Oaks, CA: Sage.

Organista, K. C. (2006). Cognitive-behavioral therapy with Latinos and Latinas. In P. A. Hays & G. Y. Iwamasa (Eds.), *Culturally responsive cognitive–behavioral therapy: Assessment, practice, and supervision* (pp. 73–96). Washington, DC: American Psychological Association.

Öst, L.-G. (1997). Rapid treatment of specific phobias. In G. C. L. Davey (Ed.), *Phobias: A handbook of theory research and treatment* (pp. 227–246). New York, NY: Wiley.

Overmier, J. B., & Seligman, M. E. P. (1967). Effects of inescapable shock upon subsequent escape and avoidance responding. *Journal of Comparative and Physiological Psychology, 63*, 28–33. doi:10.1037/h0024166

Parsons, T. D., & Rizzo, A. A. (2008). Affective outcomes of virtual reality exposure therapy for anxiety and specific phobias: A meta-analysis. *Journal of Behavior Therapy and Experimental Psychiatry, 39*, 250–261. doi:10.1016/j.jbtep.2007.07.007

Pavlov, I. P. (1927). *Conditioned reflexes: An investigation of the physiological activity of the cerebral cortex*. London, England: Oxford University Press.

Pfammatter, M., Junghan, U. M., & Brenner, H. D. (2006). Efficacy of psychological therapy in schizophrenia: Conclusions from meta-analyses. *Schizophrenia Bulletin, 32*(Suppl. 1), S64–S80. doi:10.1093/schbul/sbl030

Pinquart, M., Duberstein, P. R., & Lyness, J. M. (2007). Effects of psychotherapy and other behavioral interventions on clinically depressed older adults: A meta-analysis. *Aging & Mental Health, 11*, 645–657. doi:10.1080/13607860701529635

Plaud, J. J. (2005). Covert conditioning. In M. Hersen & J. Rosqvist (Eds.), *Encyclopedia of behavior modification and cognitive behavior therapy: Vol. 1. Adult clinical applications* (pp. 235–241). Thousand Oaks, CA: Sage.

Poling, A., & Gaynor, S. T. (2009). Stimulus control. In W. T. O'Donohue & J. E. Fisher (Eds.), *General principles and empirically supported principles of cognitive behavior therapy* (pp. 600–607). Hoboken, NJ: Wiley.

Powers, M. B., Vedel, E., & Emmelkamp, P. M. G. (2008). Behavioral couples therapy (BCT) for alcohol and drug use disorders: A meta-analysis. *Clinical Psychology Review, 28,* 952–962. doi:10.1016/j.cpr.2008.02.002

Premack, D. (1965). Reinforcement theory. In D. Levine (Ed.), *Nebraska Symposium on Motivation* (pp. 123–180). Lincoln: University of Nebraska Press.

Reger, M. A., & Gahm, G. A. (2009). A meta-analysis of the effects of Internet- and computer-based cognitive-behavioral treatments for anxiety. *Journal of Clinical Psychology, 65,* 53–75. doi:10.1002/jclp.20536

Rescorla, R. A. (1988). Pavlovian conditioning: It's not what you think it is. *American Psychologist, 43,* 151–160. doi:10.1037/0003-066X.43.3.151

Rescorla, R. A., & Wagner, A. R. (1972). A theory of Pavlovian conditioning: Variations in the effectiveness of reinforcement and nonreinforcement. In A. H. Black & W. F. Prokasy (Eds.), *Classical conditioning II: Current research and theory* (pp. 64–99). New York, NY: Appleton Century Crofts.

Robie, W. F. (1925). *The art of love.* Ithaca, NY: Rational Life Press.

Roemer, L., & Orsillo, S. M. (2009). *Mindfulness- and acceptance-based behavioral therapies in practice.* New York, NY: Guilford Press.

Rollnick, S., Miller, W. R., & Butler, C. C. (2008). *Motivational interviewing in health care: Helping patients change behavior.* New York, NY: Guilford Press.

Rosa-Alcázar, A. I., Sánchez-Meca, J., Gómez-Conesa, A., & Marín-Martínez, F. (2008). Psychological treatment of obsessive-compulsive disorder: A meta-analysis. *Clinical Psychology Review, 28,* 1310–1325. doi:10.1016/j.cpr.2008.07.001

Rosen, G. M., & Davison, G. C. (2003). Psychology should list empirically supported principles of change (ESPs) and not credential trademarked therapies or other treatment packages. *Behavior Modification, 27,* 300–312. doi:10.1177/0145445503027003003

Rosengren, D. B. (2009). *Building motivational interviewing skills: A practitioner workbook.* New York, NY: Guilford Press.

Rowa, K., Antony, M. M., & Swinson, R. P. (2007). Exposure and ritual prevention. In M. M. Antony, C. Purdon, & L. J. Summerfeldt (Eds.), *Psychological treatment of OCD: Fundamentals and beyond* (pp. 79–109). Washington, DC: American Psychological Association. doi:10.1037/11543-004

Rush, A. J., First, M. B., & Blacker, D. (Eds.). (2008). *Handbook of psychiatric measures* (2nd ed.). Washington, DC: American Psychiatric Association.

Safran, J. D., Muran, J. C., Samstag, L. W., & Stevens, C. (2002). Repairing alliance ruptures. In J. C. Norcross (Ed.), *Psychotherapy relationships that work: Ther-*

apist contributions and responsiveness to patients (pp. 235–254). New York, NY: Oxford University Press.

Sánchez-Meca, J., Rosa-Alcárez, A. I., Marín-Martínez, F., & Gómez-Conesa, A. (2010). Psychological treatment of panic disorder with or without agoraphobia: A meta-analysis. *Clinical Psychology Review, 30,* 37–50. doi:10.1016/j.cpr.2009.08.011

Santiago-Rivera, A., Kanter, J., Benson, G., Derose, T., Illes, R., & Reyes, W. (2008). Behavioral activation as an alternative treatment approach for Latinos with depression. *Psychotherapy: Theory, Research, Practice, Training, 45,* 173–185. doi:10.1037/0033-3204.45.2.173

Savard, J., Savard, M. H., & Morin, C. M. (2010). Insomnia. In M. M. Antony & D. H. Barlow (Eds.), *Handbook of assessment and treatment planning psychological disorders* (2nd ed.; pp. 633–669). New York, NY: Guilford Press.

Segal, Z. V., Williams, J. M. G., & Teasdale, J. D. (2002). *Mindfulness-based cognitive therapy for depression: A new approach to preventing relapse.* New York, NY: Guilford Press.

Segrin, C. (2009). Social skills training. In W. T. O'Donohue & J. E. Fisher (Eds.), *General principles and empirically supported principles of cognitive behavior therapy* (pp. 600–607). Hoboken, NJ: Wiley.

Shapiro, S. L., Carlson, L. E., Astin, J. A., & Freedman, B. (2006). Mechanisms of mindfulness. *Journal of Clinical Psychology, 62,* 373–386. doi:10.1002/jclp.20237

Skinner, B. F. (1938). *The behavior of organisms.* New York, NY: Appleton-Century.

Society of Clinical Psychology. (2010). *Website on research-supported psychological treatments.* Retrieved from http://www.psychology.sunysb.edu/eklonsky-/division12/index.html

Spiegler, M. D., & Guevremont, D. C. (2010). *Contemporary behavior therapy* (5th ed.). Belmont, CA: Wadsworth Cengage Learning.

Stern, R., & Marks, I. (1973). Brief and prolonged flooding: A comparison in agoraphobic patients. *Archives of General Psychiatry, 28,* 270–276.

Stewart, R. E., & Chambless, D. L. (2009). Cognitive behavioral therapy for adult anxiety disorders in clinical practice: A meta-analysis of effectiveness studies. *Journal of Consulting and Clinical Psychology, 77,* 595–606. doi:10.1037/a0016032

Sue, S. (1998). In search of cultural competence in psychotherapy and counseling. *American Psychologist, 53,* 440–448. doi:10.1037/0003-066X.53.4.440

Sue, S. (2006). Cultural competency: From philosophy to research and practice. *Journal of Community Psychology, 34,* 237–245. doi:10.1002/jcop.20095

Swartz, H. A., Zuckoff, A., Grote, N. K., Spielvogle, H. N., Bledsoe, S. E., Shear, M. K., & Frank, E. (2007). Engaging depressed patients in psychotherapy: Integrating techniques from motivational interviewing and ethnographic interviewing to improve treatment participation. *Professional Psychology: Research and Practice, 38,* 430–439. doi:10.1037/0735-7028.38.4.430

Swinson, R. P., Antony, M. M., Bleau, P., Chokka, P., Craven, M., Fallu, A., . . . Walker, J. R. (2006). Clinical practice guidelines: Management of anxiety disorders. *Canadian Journal of Psychiatry, 51*(Suppl. 2), 1S–92S. Retrieved from http://publications.cpa-apc.org/browse/documents/213&xwm=true

Tanaka-Matsumi, J., Seiden, D. Y., & Lam, K. N. (1996). The Culturally Informed Functional Assessment (CIFA) Interview: A strategy for cross-cultural behavioral practice. *Cognitive and Behavioral Practice, 3,* 215–233. doi:10.1016/S1077-7229(96)80015-0

Task Force on Promotion and Dissemination of Psychological Procedures. (1995). Training in and dissemination of empirically validated treatments: Report and recommendations. *Clinical Psychologist, 48*(1), 3–23.

Taylor, S. (2000). *Understanding and treating panic disorder: Cognitive-behavioural approaches.* Chichester, England: Wiley.

Teasdale, J. D., Moore, R. G., Hayhurst, H., Pope, M., Williams, S., & Segal, Z. V. (2002). Metacognitive awareness and prevention of relapse in depression: Empirical evidence. *Journal of Consulting and Clinical Psychology, 70,* 275–287. doi:10.1037/0022-006X.70.2.275

Thorndike, E. L. (1911). *Animal intelligence: Experimental studies.* New York, NY: Macmillan.

Tolin, D. F., Diefenbach, G. J., Maltby, N., & Hannan, S. (2005). Stepped care for obsessive compulsive disorder: A pilot study. *Cognitive and Behavioral Practice, 12,* 403–414. doi:10.1016/S1077-7229(05)80068-9

Tryon, W. W. (2005). Possible mechanisms for why desensitization and exposure therapy work. *Clinical Psychology Review, 25,* 67–95. doi:10.1016/j.cpr.2004.08.005

Turner, S. M., Johnson, M. R., Beidel, D. C., Heiser, N. A., & Lydiard, R. B. (2003). The Social Thoughts and Beliefs Scale: A new inventory for assessing cognitions in social phobia. *Psychological Assessment, 15,* 384–391. doi:10.1037/1040-3590.15.3.384

Vittengl, J. R., Clark, L. A., Dunn, T. W., & Jarrett, R. B. (2007). Reducing relapse and recurrence in unipolar depression: A comparative meta-analysis of cognitive behavioral therapy's effects. *Journal of Consulting and Clinical Psychology, 75,* 475–488. doi:10.1037/0022-006X.75.3.475

Wacker, D. P., Harding, J., Berg, W., Cooper-Brown, L. J., & Barretto, A. (2009). Punishment. In W. T. O'Donohue & J. E. Fisher (Eds.), *General principles and empirically supported techniques of cognitive behavior therapy* (pp. 506–512). Hoboken, NJ: Wiley.

Wallace, M. D., & Najdowski, A. C. (2009). Differential reinforcement of other behavior and differential reinforcement of alternative behavior. In W. T. O'Donohue & J. E. Fisher (Eds.), *General principles and empirically supported techniques of cognitive behavior therapy* (pp. 245–255). Hoboken, NJ: Wiley.

Wang, P. S., Lane, M., Olfson, M., Pincus, H. A., Wells, K. B., & Kessler, R. C. (2005). Twelve-month use of mental health services in the United States: Results from the National Comorbidity Survey Replication. *Archives of General Psychiatry, 62,* 629–640. doi:10.1001/archpsyc.62.6.629

Watson, J. B. (1913). Psychology as the behaviorist views it. *Psychological Review, 20,* 158–177. doi:10.1037/h0074428

Watson, J. B., & Raynor, R. (1920). Conditioned emotional reactions. *Journal of Experimental Psychology, 3,* 1–14. doi:10.1037/h0069608

Wechsler, D. (2008). *WAIS–IV administration and scoring manual.* San Antonio, TX: Pearson Assessment.

Weisz, J. R., McCarty, C. A., & Valeri, S. M. (2006). Effects of psychotherapy for depression in children and adolescents: A meta-analysis. *Psychological Bulletin, 132,* 132–149. doi:10.1037/0033-2909.132.1.132

Westra, H. A., Dozois, D. J. A., & Marcus, M. (2007). Expectancy, homework compliance, and initial change in cognitive-behavioral therapy for anxiety. *Journal of Consulting and Clinical Psychology, 75,* 363–373. doi:10.1037/0022-006X. 75.3.363

Wilson, G. T. (1998). Manual-based treatment and clinical practice [Review]. *Clinical Psychology: Science and Practice, 5,* 363–375. doi:10.1111/j.1468-2850. 1998.tb00156.x

Wilson, G. T., & Fairburn, C. G. (2007). Treatments for eating disorders. In P. E. Nathan & J. M. Gorman (Eds.), *A guide to treatments that work* (3rd ed., pp. 581–583). New York, NY: Oxford University Press.

Wilson, K. G., & Murrell, A. R. (2004). Values work in acceptance and commitment therapy. In S. C. Hayes, V. M. Follette, & M. M. Linehan (Eds.), *Mindfulness and acceptance: Expanding the cognitive-behavioral tradition* (pp. 120–151). New York, NY: Guilford Press.

Wilson, K. G., Sandoz, E. K., Flynn, M. K., Slater, R., & DuFrene, T. (2010). Understanding, assessing, and treating values processes in mindfulness and acceptance-based therapies. In R. Baer (Ed.), *Assessing mindfulness and acceptance: Illuminating the processes of change* (pp. 77–106). Oakland, CA: New Harbinger.

Witkiewitz, K., & Aracelliz Villarroel, N. (2009). Dynamic association between negative affect and alcohol lapses following alcohol treatment. *Journal of Consulting and Clinical Psychology, 77,* 633–644. doi:10.1037/a0015647

Witt, J. C., & Elliott, S. N. (1983). Assessment in behavioral consultation: The initial interview. *School Psychology Review, 12,* 42–49.

Wolitzky-Taylor, K. B., Horowitz, J. D., Powers, M. B., & Telch, M. J. (2008). Psychological approaches in the treatment of specific phobias: A meta-analysis. *Clinical Psychology Review, 28,* 1021–1037. doi:10.1016/j.cpr.2008.02.007

Wolpe, J. (1952). Experimental neuroses as learned behavior. *British Journal of Psychology, 43,* 243–268.

Wolpe, J. (1958). *Psychotherapy by reciprocal inhibition.* Stanford, CA: Stanford University Press.

Wolpe, J. (1997). Thirty years of behavior therapy. *Behavior Therapy, 28,* 633–635. doi:10.1016/S0005-7894(97)80023-8

Wolpe, J., Salter, A., & Reyna, L. J. (Eds.). (1964). *The conditioning therapies: The challenge of psychotherapy.* New York, NY: Holt, Rinehart & Winston.

Wood, J. M., Nezworski, M. T., Lilienfeld, S. O., & Garb, H. N. (2003). *What's wrong with the Rorschach? Science confronts the controversial inkblot test.* Hoboken, NJ: Wiley.

Wykes, T., Steel, C., Everitt, B., & Tarrier, N. (2007). Cognitive behavior therapy for schizophrenia: Effect sizes, clinical models, and methodological rigor. *Schizophrenia Bulletin, 34,* 523–537. doi:10.1093/schbul/sbm114

Yartz, A. R., & Hawk, L. W. (2001). Psychophysiological assessment of anxiety: Tales from the heart. In M. M. Antony, S. M. Orsillo, & L. Roemer (Eds.), *Practitioner's guide to empirically-based measures of anxiety* (pp. 25–30). New York, NY: Springer.

Young, K. M., Northern, J. J., Lister, K. M., Drummond, J. A., & O'Brien, W. H. (2007). A meta-analysis of family-behavioral weight-loss treatments for children. *Clinical Psychology Review, 27,* 240–249. doi:10.1016/j.cpr.2006.08.003

Zaretsky, A., Lancee, W., Miller, C., Harris, A., & Parikh, S. V. (2008). Is cognitive-behavioural therapy more effective than psychoeducation in bipolar disorder? *Canadian Journal of Psychiatry, 53,* 441–448.

Zwahlen, M., Renehan, A., & Egger, M. (2008). Meta-analysis in medical research: Potentials and limitations. *Urologic Oncology: Seminars and Original Investigations, 26,* 320–329. doi:10.1016/j.urolonc.2006.12.001

Index

About the Authors

Martin M. Antony, Phd, ABPP, is professor and graduate program director in the Department of Psychology at Ryerson University in Toronto. He is also director of research at the Anxiety Treatment and Research Centre at St. Joseph's Healthcare in Hamilton, Ontario, Canada, and past president of the Canadian Psychological Association. He was founding director of both the Anxiety Treatment and Research Centre and the Psychology Residency Program at St. Joseph's Healthcare. He was also a psychologist at the Centre for Addiction and Mental Health in Toronto and assistant professor of psychiatry at the University of Toronto.

Dr. Antony received his PhD in clinical psychology from the University at Albany, State University of New York, in 1994, and completed his internship at the University of Mississippi Medical Center. He has published 28 books, including a variety of evidence-based self-help manuals (e.g., *Anti-Anxiety Workbook; Shyness and Social Anxiety Workbook* [2nd ed.]; *When Perfect Isn't Good Enough* [2nd ed.]), clinical guides to assessment and treatment (e.g., *Cognitive-Behavioral Therapy in Groups; Phobic Disorders and Panic in Adults*), and research texts (e.g., *Obsessive Compulsive Disorder; Oxford Handbook of Anxiety and Related Disorders*). In addition, Dr. Antony has published more than 150 scientific articles and book chapters in the areas of cognitive–behavioral therapy, obsessive–compulsive disorder, panic disorder, social phobia, specific phobia, perfectionism, and related topics.

Dr. Antony has received career awards from the Society of Clinical Psychology (Division 12 of the American Psychological Association), the

Canadian Psychological Association, and the Anxiety Disorders Association of America and is a fellow of the American and Canadian Psychological Associations. He has also served on the boards of directors for the Society of Clinical Psychology and the Association for Behavioral and Cognitive Therapies and as program chair for past conventions of the Association for Behavioral and Cognitive Therapies and the Anxiety Disorders Association of America. Dr. Antony also served as an advisor to the *DSM–IV* Text Revision Work Group for Anxiety Disorders.

Lizabeth Roemer, PhD, is a professor of psychology at the University of Massachusetts Boston, where she is actively involved in research and clinical training of doctoral students in clinical psychology. Dr. Roemer received her BA from Northwestern University and her MS and PhD from the Pennsylvania State University and completed her internship and postdoctoral fellowship at the National Center for PTSD at the Boston Veterans Affairs Healthcare System.

In collaboration with Dr. Susan Orsillo, Dr. Roemer has developed an acceptance-based behavior therapy for generalized anxiety disorder and is currently examining its efficacy and mediators and moderators of change in a study funded by the National Institute of Mental Health. She and Dr. Orsillo coauthored the clinical guide *Mindfulness and Acceptance-Based Behavioral Therapies in Practice,* as well as the evidence-based self-help guide *The Mindful Way Through Anxiety: Breaking Free From Worry and Reclaiming Your Life;* coedited the research text *Acceptance and Mindfulness-Based Approaches to Anxiety: New Directions in Conceptualization and Treatment;* and regularly present workshops on acceptance-based behavior therapies. In addition, Dr. Roemer has published more than 70 journal articles and book chapters in the areas of behavior therapy, generalized anxiety disorder, posttraumatic stress disorder, mindfulness, experiential avoidance, emotion regulation, and related areas.

About the Series Editors

Jon Carlson, PsyD, EdD, ABPP, is distinguished professor of psychology and counseling at Governors State University in University Park, Illinois, and a psychologist at the Wellness Clinic in Lake Geneva, Wisconsin. Dr. Carlson has served as the editor of several periodicals, including the *Journal of Individual Psychology* and *The Family Journal.* He holds diplomas in both family psychology and Adlerian psychology. He has authored 150 journal articles and 40 books, including *Time for a Better Marriage, Adlerian Therapy, The Mummy at the Dining Room Table, Bad Therapy, The Client Who Changed Me,* and *Moved by the Spirit.* He has created more than 200 professional trade videos and DVDs with leading professional therapists and educators. In 2004 the American Counseling Association named him a "Living Legend." Recently he syndicated an advice cartoon *On The Edge* with cartoonist Joe Martin.

Matt Englar-Carlson, PhD, is an associate professor of counseling at California State University, Fullerton. He is a fellow of Division 51 of the American Psychological Association (APA). As a scholar, teacher, and clinician, Dr. Englar-Carlson has been an innovator and is professionally passionate about training and teaching clinicians to work more effectively with their male clients. He has more than 30 publications and 50 national and international presentations, most of which are focused on men and masculinity and diversity issues in psychological training and practice. Dr. Englar-Carlson coedited the books *In the Room With Men: A Casebook* *of Therapeutic Change* and *Counseling Troubled Boys: A Guidebook for Professionals,* and was featured in the 2010 APA Psychotherapy series DVD *Engaging Men in Psychotherapy.* In 2007 he was named the Researcher of the Year by the Society for the Psychological Study of Men and Masculinity. He is also a member of the APA Working Group to Develop Guidelines for Psychological Practice With Boys and Men. As a clinician, he has worked with children, adults, and families in school, community, and university mental health settings.